El Alamein 1942

The Axis' Major Defeat in Africa

El Alamein 1942

The Axis' Major Defeat in Africa

D. STAVROPOULOS - S. VOURLIOTIS - K. PARATHIRAS - J. TERNIOTIS
CH. NIKOLAOU - D. GEDEON - N. PANOS

"The Desert Fox" by David Pentland.

AUTHORS
D. Stavropoulos - S. Vourliotis - K. Parathiras
J. Terniotis - Ch. Nikolaou - D. Gedeon - N. Panos

EDITORS (ENGLISH EDITION)
Nikos Giannopoulos, *Historian*
Stelios Demiras

TRANSLATOR
Alexis Mehtidis

PROOF EDITOR
Charles Davis

COVER ART
David Pentland- published by permission
of Craston Fine Arts.
(www.davidpentland.com)

UNIFORM RESEARCH AND COLOR PLATES
Nicholas A. Panos

AIRCRAFT PROFILES
Richard J. Caruana

AFV PROFILES
Dimitris Hadoulas

ART DIRECTOR AND COVER DESIGN
Dimitra Mitsou

MAPS
Nicholas A. Panos

PICTURE CREDITS
Bunderarchiv, US Archives, Authors' Archives,
Periscopio Publications' Collection

First published in Greece in 2008
by Periscopio Publications
in cooperation with Squadron/Signal Publications

Distributed worldwide exclusively
by Squadron/Signal Publications
1115 Crowley Drive
Carrollton, TX 75006-1312 U.S.A.
www.SquadronSignalPublications.com

© 2008 Periscopio Publications

ISBN: 978-0-89747-563-1

DIMITRIOS STAVROPOULOS
Dimitrios Stavropoulos is a graduate
mechanical engineer and works in the Greek
defense industry. He has published a series of
articles on military history since 1996 and has
edited 20 books in the Greek language.

KONSTANTINOS N. PARATHIRAS
Konstantinos N. Parathiras was born in
Athens in 1969. He graduated from the
Anavryta Classical Lyceum and then studied
Law, Economics and Political Science in the
National and Kapodistrian University of
Athens. Post-graduate studies on Civil Law
followed in the same university. He served in
the Hellenic Air Force as a reserve officer
after his studies. He initially worked as a
lawyer and, then, in the Court of Auditors
from 1998. He has been writing articles for
Periscopio Publications since 1999. His main
hobby is small weapons.

NICHOLAS A. PANOS
Born in Athens in 1961 where he still lives
and works. Studied art, graphic and product
design. Since 1981 he's been working as a
free-lance designer and illustrator for
advertising agencies, publishing houses in
Europe and the U.S.A. During his military
service in the Hellenic Navy, he designed and
illustrated the present official Uniform
Regulations Manual. (He is currently a
special consultant and a member of the
Maritime Museum of Greece) The experience
he's thus acquired — in conjunction with his
predilection for historical and military

subjects — is being applied since 1999 in
designing and illustrating magazine covers,
maps and insignia. He has illustrated over 45
history book/album titles.

SOTIRIS VOURLIOTIS
Sotiris Vourliotis was born in Athens in 1968.
He studied in the Department of Mechanical
Engineering of the Chalkis Technological
Educational Institution and then in the
School of Mechanical Engineering of the
National Technical University of Athens.
He works as a public works designer.
He has written articles for the Periscopio
Publications' military history and defence
magazines since 2000 and has dealt with
various subjects, mostly of the World War II
period for which he has been interested since
his school years.

JOHN TERNIOTIS
John Terniotis was born in Athens on
September 1952 and studied Aircraft
Engineering. After some years of military
service with the Hellenic Army Armoured
Corps, he joined Civil Aviation and still works
as Maintenance Operations Chief Inspector.
He has written several articles on Military
History issues, and performed photographic
research in WWII battlefields, airfields and
other sites in Greece. His hobby is Aviation
Archaeology. He owns a collection of several
relics of Luftwaffe and Regia Aeronautica
aircraft and items found in areas used by the
Axis forces during WWII.

DIMITRIOS GEDEON
Dimitrios Gedeon is a Major General
(retired). He is a graduate of Hellenic Army
Military Academy (Class of 1960) and
Hellenic Armed Forces National Defense
School. He served in the Hellenic Army from
1960 to 1989 and has been a teacher of
Military History in the Hellenic Army
Military Academy from 1994 to 1997,
Assistant Director of the Hellenic Army
History Directorate and Secretary to the
Hellenic Military History Commission from
1997 to 1999. He has written two books about
Hellenic Army History and a great number
of articles on Military History.

† CHARALAMBOS NIKOLAOU
Charalambos Nikolaou (Brigadier General,
Retired) was born in1924. He graduated
from the Hellenic Army Military Academy as
a Second Lieutenant (Signals) in 1948 and
took part in anti-guerilla operations in 1948-
49. He, also, graduated from the War College
and obtained his Master in Business
Administration from the Athens School of
Economics and Business. He served as a
commanding or a staff officer in various
Signals units, as a formations' staff officer
in the Hellenic Army General Staff and in
SHAPE (Belgium). He retired in 1975, but
returned and served in the Army History
Directorate as a writer. He was, also, a
Military History Teacher in the Hellenic
Army Military Academy. He died in 2004.

Contents

Preface

The exhausted British forces in charge of conducting war in the North African desert were in retreat in all sectors, unable to oppose the "Rommel phenomenon" in the summer of 1942. The Africa Corps panzers quickly reached positions two hours from Alexandria, creating a justified spirit of euphoria in the German leadership. Hitler's almost utopian goals seemed provocatively within easy reach. Seizing Egypt seemed just a matter of time with multiple consequences for the course of the war. Syria, Palestine, the strategic encirclement of Turkey, and the exposure of the suffering Soviet Union's southern front would follow. The last obstacle on the road to Alexandria was the 8th British Army, that stopped after a long retreat at the El Alamein railroad station. The disciplined British troops and their hardened allies would stand for their last defense there, under General Bernard Law Montgomery. Rommel attacked violently, but he did not manage to overcome the stubborn defense of his opponents. After a bloody 12-day battle, the Africa Corps was forced to retreat. The legendary 8th Army had broken up the German dreams for the domination of North Africa in the most emphatic way and had given Britain its last victory as a great independent world power.

Nikos Giannopoulos
Editor

The Battle of El Alamein

A methodical victory

In the summer of 1942, the British 8th Army was determined not to yield a further inch when it reached the small, insignificant coastal railroad station of El Alamein closely pursued by the Axis forces. The man who could the army believe again in its capabilities and could lead it to victory was found at the most opportune moment and by a strange stroke of fate. Field Marshal Erwin Rommel's Panzer Army, which hung like the sword of Damocles over Suez, was routed, and the war in North Africa was decided.

Field Marshal Rommel at El Alamein on 28 October 1942 discusses the battle situation with the commanding officer of the 21st Panzer Division in front of his Kampfstaffel. This advanced headquarters comprised a radio-equipped PzKpfw III, a SdKfz 232 radio-equipped armored car, Rommel's personal SdKfz 250/3 "Greif" half-track, and some captured British Honey light tanks. (The "Desert Fox" by David Pentland, published by permission of Cranston Fine Arts - www.davidpentland.com)

A German PzKpfw III moves at high speed in the desert.

1 July 1942 marked the worst possible omen for the fortunes of the British Empire in Egypt. A pall of smoke hung over the Middle East Command Headquarters near the banks of the Nile. It was the result of the burning by the headquarters staff of huge quantities of classified documents to prevent them falling into the hands of the enemy, an enemy that was advancing without hindrance. The leave of all British 8th Army (the command that was waging war in the Western Desert) personnel was cancelled and a curfew was enforced for the first time since the beginning of the war. The Royal Navy's Mediterranean Fleet evacuated its Alexandria base, the roads were full of Royal Engineers preparing to blow up key installations, and the trains heading for Palestine were heavily laden with panic-stricken crowds, pushing and shoving to secure a place heading for safety, away from the German panzers that were getting close. Part of the American Military Mission was already leaving for safety in Khartoum and Asmara, while even King Farouk, who had especially good relations with the British, was getting

ready to abandon his capital. The Egyptians went about their business with their usual stoicism and fatalism, attributing the developing situation to "Allah's will." They did not have any special reason to dislike the Germans, who preached anti-Semitism and were helping the Arab liberation movements at every opportunity, although they preferred the British, who had taken care of the defense of the country since 1882.

The "tidal wave" that brought Field Marshall Erwin Rommel's Panzer Army Africa (Panzerarmee Afrika) to the gates of Cairo began with the overwhelming defeat of the Allied armies in May and June at the Battle of Gazala. The British failure to

General Sir Harold Alexander, commander-in-chief, Middle East Command from August 1942. A man of great merit, he distinguished himself as a divisional commander at Dunkirk and as general officer, commander-in-chief, Southern Command, one of the most important commands in Britain, for more than a year. Also, in Burma from February 1942, when he showed the same virtues of self-control and sound judgment while directing the retreat.

The Allied retreat finally halted, and these Australian soldiers take the opportunity to write a letter home from the El Alamein "heaven."

hold an almost untenable front along its southern side was followed by the quick fall of the port of Tobruk, with its accompanying loss of huge quantities of supplies and at least 30,000 prisoners falling into the hands of the Germans. This success brought Rommel a field marshal's baton. After the fall of Tobruk, the positions the exhausted 8th Army later attempted to defend were in danger of being overrun as it ceded space to its adversary in order to gain time. General Claude Auchinleck, the commander-in-chief Middle East, personally took command of the 8th Army, and attempted but failed to check the Germans' swift advance to Mersah Matruh. So, on 1 July, Rommel's advance guards reached the El Alamein position that at that moment was, more or less, unfortified and seemed ready to succumb to the enemy – like Gazala before it.

The disciplined British soldiers and their allies would surely fight stubbornly, but, if the Germans attacked with the same ferocity they had shown at Tobruk, they would most probably succeed in breaking through the Allied lines after which nothing could stop them. The

Supreme Command (OKW) of German Armed Forces, as well as other senior German officers, never openly admitted to any specific plan for Nazi world domination or for the Afrika Korps to link up with the armies operating in the Caucasus. However, in the summer of 1942, the fact remains that these ambitious goals had every chance of success. Alexandria was a mere two hours away for the panzers, and the road to Cairo was open. If Egypt were seized by Rommel's Panzer Army, Malta and the whole of the Mediterranean basin would be lost forever for the Allies, and the Suez Canal – with its huge depots – would bring for the Germans "booty equivalent to 50 Tobruks," according to British war correspondents. It would be impossible to hold Palestine and Syria and, when Rommel reached Jerusalem and Damascus, Iraq's oil would also be his. Turkey would also be strategically surrounded, thus leaving the Soviet Union's southern flank exposed. Finally, the Red Sea would succumb to Axis domination and India, already under threat from the Japanese advancing from the east, would have to face a new, more dangerous foe from the west.

German and Italian morale was definitely higher than that of the Allies, who were struggling to save their last bastions in the Eastern Mediterranean. Rommel's men were driven by an ambition of new conquests and rewards and by the pride they had gained from their successes. On the other hand, the British were fighting with the knowledge that this was their last chance, and if they were beaten in El Alamein, the defeat would be final. Surprisingly, the German attacks at the beginning of July 1942 were not as forceful as expected and were not characterized by Rommel's usual aggressiveness. British positions held on 4 July and continued to do so throughout the next day. By the month's second week, the defenders had consolidated their positions and it looked as though they would hold on to this narrow front with stubborn resistance. It was here that General Auchinleck would fight the most important battle of his life during the following days, driving back Rommel's penetrations and launching his own counterattacks, like a swordsman who first parries and then lunges. However, he did not forget to prepare plans for a further withdrawal as, according to him, "if the Nile Delta is lost, I can hope that I will, sometime, get it back, but, if the 8th Army is lost, I lose everything."

It was the Axis forces' complicated command system that played a decisive role in checking their advance. Rommel, as Panzer Army Africa commander, was subordinate to the Italian Supreme Command (Comando Supremo). Its chief was Field Marshal (Feldmaresciallo) Ugo Cavallero, and Lieutenant General

(General der Infanterie) Enno von Rintelen was attached to it as a military attaché and OKW representative. Field Marshal Albert Kesselring was also in Italy as commander-in-chief of all German air forces in the Mediterranean theater, and Rommel was formally his subordinate, according to German hierarchy. In reality, however, Rommel received his orders directly from the OKW, and these were often different from those issued by the Italians. Rommel used this situation for his own benefit, in spite of complaining publicly about it, until Italian inactivity cut his supply flow.

In reality, El Alamein was an insignificant dusty railroad station close to the Mediterranean coast, 225 kilometers from the hubbub of Cairo and 90 kilometers from cosmopolitan Alexandria. There were excellent tactical reasons that dictated to Auchinleck, a highly competent general, that the El Alamein position

General Georg Stumme assumed command of Panzer Army Africa after Rommel was taken ill. Rommel had openly professed that he would have preferred Heinz Guderian, considered the foremost expert in armored warfare, as his replacement.

German gunners reposition one of the Deutsches Afrika Korps' (DAK) lethal 88 mm anti-aircraft guns. The white rings on the barrel denote British tanks destroyed by this particular weapon. The "88" was one of the Germans' main assets in North Africa, as it was also used as an anti-tank gun with outstanding results, "passing through our tanks as if they were made of butter," as one British tank officer commander commented.

A British crew of a Grant tank enjoy a short tea break in the desert. The 8th Army was supplied with Grants by the United States and they bridged, somehow, the qualitative gap between British armor and the German panzers, as their main armament was a 75 mm main gun with a 37mm secondary armament. Their drawbacks were the hull's architecture that gave the main gun a very short arc of traverse and their relatively tall silhouette.

was the place to reorganize his army and check the enemy's advance. According to a succinct comment by a British observer, "That place (El Alamein) was the only one in the North African desert that possessed a bottom and a top." All other defensive lines that the British, Germans, or Italians had tried to hold during the previous two years had, inevitably, the fairly secure Mediterranean Sea as its northern flank and the vastness of the Sahara as its southern one, making any front exposed as it allowed any outflanking maneuver to take advantage of this gap. The El Alamein line, on the other hand, was just 60 kilometers wide and was bordered in the south by a "geographical oddity": the Qattara Depression, a huge rhomboid area, 210 kilometers long and 110 kilometers wide, with a surface that was, in places, below sea-level. The desert at this point is interrupted by a steep escarpment 300 meters high with a flat surface, and surrounded by almost vertical "banks." It is believed to have once been an inland sea that had dried out over time, as there is plenty of salt there. The German reconnaissance detachments that reached its edges could not make out its bottom as it was lost in a pink haze. The Qattara Depression had been mapped a few

years earlier and was considered impassable. Its surface consisted of soft sand, covered by a thin, salty crust that could stand the weight of one man but not that of a vehicle. Any wheeled vehicle that tried to cross it slowly sank and was completely swallowed. The local Bedouins knew only two dangerous tracks through it that could stand the weight of a camel or a truck but, with the exception of the British Long Range Desert Group (LRDG's) daring reconnaissance operations, no other European had successfully attempted to cross it. Another formidable barrier extended from the northwestern corner of this "marsh" to the Siwa Oasis, to the west, while, to the south, for hundreds of kilometers, lay the Great Sand Sea.

For this reason, the Germans and Italians had to approach the British positions from the coastal road, as the Qattara Depression progressively narrowed, causing a bottleneck to the north, with El Alamein at its narrowest point. Middle East Headquarters was aware of the great strategic significance of the area so, when the retreating 8th Army reached the area, the 9th Australian Division, which had been urgently recalled from Syria, was already manning some fortifications that had been hastily built. These Australians were the renowned Tobruk defenders of 1941, the "Desert Rats," men from sunburnt their long service in the Middle East, fresh from many months of guard duties, "ready to rush into battle, with their muscles like tennis balls" as described by a BBC correspondent. Despite many attempts throughout July, the Germans were unable to dislodge the "Aussies." As the British said, "It was a 'match ball' for Rommel, who had won all previous sets, but he was unable to win those extra points." What took place at El Alamein had occurred

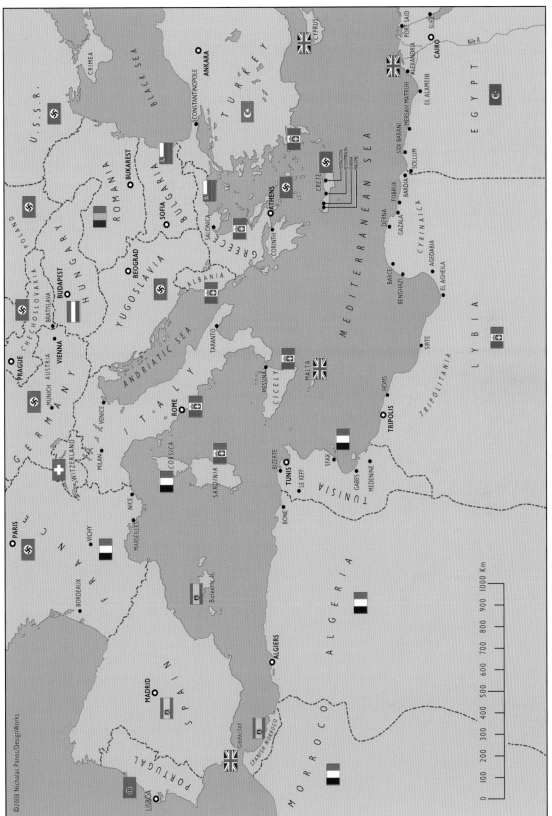

The geopolitical situation in Europe and North Africa in October 1942. (Map design: Nicholas Panos)

before many times in the North African Campaign. The few weeks of intense action, at Sidi Barani, Sollum, Aghedabia and Gazala, had been followed by a few weeks of rest, reorganization and stockpiling of supplies. The side that could complete its preparations first would strike first. However, after sacrificing 13,000 men in July, the 8th Army had held its positions and Egypt was saved.

The 8th Army and the Afrika Korps

What were the reasons that the 8th Army found itself on the defensive, with its back to the wall? Britain had been fighting the war alone for quite some time and, during that time, had been forced to produce as many weapons as possible at the expense of quality. Most of the time, her forces in North Africa fielded the same number of tanks as Rommel but, while the German tank guns were effective up to 1,500 meters, the British guns could barely reach 1,000 meters. However, when the 8th Army began taking delivery of the American Grants, a near equilibrium of tank forces was restored, although the gap in anti-tank

Germans laid 445,358 mines in front of their forward positions during September and October 1942, hoping that they would help in repulsing the expected 8th Army attack.

guns remained in favor of the Germans.

The famous German 88 mm anti-aircraft gun, with its superbly trained crews, the king of the battlefield, while the comparable British 6-pdr guns were very few in number, that is until the summer of 1942. At the same time, the RAF possessed very few Spitfires, the main body of its fighters being made up of obsolete Hurricanes, Tomahawks and Kittyhawks, which were unable to compete with the faster German Messerschmitt 109s piloted by some of the finest aviators of all time. The Germans had developed a tank recovery and repair system that was far superior to the British, partly due to the fact that they used only two or three basic types of armored vehicles, while the 8th Army used seven. The Panzer Army Africa's petrol oil, and lubricants supply system had been greatly simplified by the use of a common 5-gallon canister that was easy and practical to carry. The Allies marched into battle knowing that they would be facing an opponent with better weapons, but each British general had to fight with the means he possessed.

In terms of tactical and command issues, Rommel did not display any ingenuity in anything original, in contrast to the myth that surrounded him in the western press. He continued to command his troops from his headquarters close to the front, and was skillful in reading changes in the battle, often reacting immediately to them, but he had committed terrible errors in his assessment of his opponents. On the other hand, the fundamental level of professionalism of the German fighting soldier was a basic factor that gave the Axis forces a qualitative supremacy. The Germans managed the coordination of air force

operations with the army's needs almost to perfection, while taking great care in minimizing bureaucracy. They were not afraid of taking responsibility and revealed a remarkable organizational capacity that always puzzled the British. The Germans were virtuosos in tank command and control. Tank crews were the Afrika Korps' elite troops, a perfectly trained team that cooperated in harmony with the anti-tank guns, always creating unpleasant surprises for the British. The Germans had long ceased using their tanks for frontal attacks, preferring to first use infantry guns, and aircraft, leaving the tanks with the task of mopping up the battlefield. They were, to a great extent, used as psychological terror weapons, such as being used at night with their lights on or, during the day, to purposely create huge clouds of dust to deceive and frighten their opponents.

However, British commentators admitted that Afrika Korps possessed a marked advantage in its senior officers: "German generals were certainly not inferior to ours. In fact, they were quite a lot better. They committed fewer mistakes and made the correct moves more often than our generals. Rommel was more capable than any British military leader for the simple reason that he had under his command more competent troops, until, that is, El Alamein. It was a large pyramid, with each stone fitting perfectly in its position, with the most impressive stone at its apex. Naturally, people's attention was drawn to the supreme stone due to its position, but, in reality, that stone was no more important than any other stone lower in the pyramid. Each stone fulfilled its mission, whatever it was. What mattered was collective strength and mass." However, in 1942, the Axis

lacked the ability to continue to improve itself during its stay in Africa, something that characterizes an army in both peace or war. It had not unveiled any new weaponry in Africa during that summer, in comparison with the 1941 campaign, merely ensuring that it had sufficient quantities of its already proven equipment. The British, on the other hand, had integrated the more modern Grant tanks within their armored forces, the Spitfires within their air forces and introduced the 6-pdr guns. The 8th Army's high command was learning from its mistakes, albeit at a slow pace, but remained heavily burdened by the failures of the recent past. A message sent by Auchinleck to London at the end of July 1942 caused his immediate replacement, though he had only voiced the truth known to everybody: "Due to lack of means and the enemy's consolidation of his front, we have come to the conclusion that, under the present circumstances, it is unfeasible to renew our attempts to break the enemy's front or to outflank him in the south. The chance of undertaking offensive operations before the middle of September is highly improbable."

A military "Messiah"

In August 1942, two new faces arrived in Egypt to take over war in the desert. The first was General Sir

British Crusader tanks await the order to advance. Their main armament was a 2-pdr (40 mm calibre) or a 6-pdr (57 mm) gun, and while they had a good turn of speed, they were underarmored, which made them very vulnerable. The small pennants on the radio antenna were used to show chain of command within a unit or formation, identification friend or foe, rank or position indicators, and for passing visual messages or orders.

The dramatic improvements in the battle readiness of the 8th Army under Montgomery's leadership, helped by the massive American aid, showed in the highly disciplined and equipped logistics units that succeeded in recovering damaged tanks even under enemy fire.

Australian "Diggers," whose reputation as tough troops was repeatedly confirmed in the Far East, the Greek campaign, and North Africa. Shown here is the Australian crew of a 40 mm Bofors anti-aircraft gun mounted on a vehicle.

Harold Alexander, the last senior British officer to evacuate the Dunkirk beaches in 1940, considered one of Britain's most level-headed and capable military leaders of the time. Alexander replaced the unappreciated and unfortunate Auchinleck as commander-in-chief Middle East, but the most important replacement was at the head of the 8th Army. In Churchill's mind, the most obvious choice was none other than Lieutenant-General W. H. E. Gott, of whom Colonel Michael Carver said "whose mental clear-headedness, composure and soundness of judgment, in connection with his readiness to propose a course of action when all others faltered and had doubts, had turned him into the oracle, to which all others turned for advice, specially in hard times." However, Gott was exhausted from his long service in Africa, and there were many people who believed that he was not the proper choice for the 8th Army under those circumstances. In

spite of these objections, the decision was made and Gott was given the job, but fate was about to intervene. On 7 August, the aircraft carrying Gott to Cairo was attacked by two German fighters and shot down, killing the noble general.

Churchill had to choose a new commander-in-chief, and this time, the suggestion of the chief of the Imperial General Staff, General Sir Alan Brooke, prevailed. From now on, the fortunes of the 8th Army would be guided by a meticulous soldier of medium height, with a thin, nervous face who neither drank nor smoked: the 54-year-old General Bernard Law Montgomery, whose character was considered to be utterly dissimilar in every respect to the "patrician" Alexander, a fact that did not prevent them from establishing a fruitful cooperation. On 12 August, a day before formally taking up his duties, he met Alexander in his map room at General Headquarters, Cairo. Alexander gave him a single laconic order: "Go in the desert and beat Rommel." The ascetic Montgomery, who had been a divisional commander at Dunkirk and, later, general officer commanding V Corps and South-Eastern Command, took charge of such an important command for the first time in his career and was determined to work tirelessly to achieve that goal.

People living in the Middle East sensed, from the end of the summer of 1942, that the time of the great confrontation was coming, and the set question during conversation was the exact timing of 8th Army's counter-attack. Rumors spread constantly and with great rapidity from the bars of Alexandria to the tents of the huge camps that the Allies had set up on the El Alamein line. The respite following the August battles was essentially a

race by both sides to resupply and reorganize, and the Germans, very obviously, lost ground right from the beginning. Rommel's supplies had to be transported to El Alamein from the Cyrenaican ports like Tobruk, which was 450 kilometers away, and Benghazi, which was almost twice as far away, while the main port of Tripoli was 1,800 kilometers away. Eight-five percent of the trucks moving these supplies carried captured war booty, and a third were at anytime in the workshops under repair. Furthermore, they were in constant danger of attack during their long journey by RAF aircraft "on the loose," aircraft that had gained virtual air superiority because of their ever-increasing numbers and also due to the ever-improving quality of their crews. On the other hand, the seaborne Axis supply route from Italy to North Africa was becoming all the more dangerous, as British submarines and aircraft, operating from Malta, managed to sink six ships in June, seven in July, and 12 in August. These losses reduced Rommel's monthly supplies from 30,000 tons to just 6,000 tons. Despite these losses, he did manage to reinforce his armored forces with 203 new tanks, among them 73 PzKpfw III with the 50 mm gun, and 27 PzKpfw IVs with the new, long 75 mm guns.

Allied supplies, constantly forwarded to El Alamein, were, on the other hand, significant from August to October and far exceeded the tonnage that Rommel was receiving. Almost 41,000 men, 800 guns, and over 1,000 tanks arrived in Egypt. Included among the tanks were 300 brand-new 36-ton Shermans that the American president, Franklin D. Roosevelt, had promised to Churchill immediately following the tragic fall of Tobruk.

British tankers were enthusiastic about the Shermans; their 75 mm guns could hit any German tank from a longer distance, with the exception of the updated and improved PzKpfw IVs, (although the enemy possessed only a few of these). There was a certainty that the next battle would be so far-reaching and ferocious that it could not be compared with any other fought in the desert up until then. Axis forces in El Alamein had dug in well and constructed a complicated trench system that was just a few kilometers from the British positions. Their front line was short and deep, thus affording the defenders a clear advantage.

The El Alamein position was held by six infantry divisions (the Italian "Pavia," "Folgore," "Brescia," "Bologna," and "Trento") and the German 164th) along with the German Ramcke Parachute Brigade (Fallschirmjäger-Brigade "Ramcke"), while six mechanized armored divisions with the Afrika Korps as its core, made up of the 15th Panzer, 21st Panzer and 90th Light, and the three Italian "Ariete," "Trieste," and "Littorio" divisions (though the latter three were of dubious fighting quality) would operate as a mobile reserve to check and repulse any local enemy penetrations. It was an open secret that Rommel could only rely on the 53,000 Germans of his Army, whom he took great care to distribute among the Italian units in order to hold together his mixed force. However, the main feature of the Axis positions

Deutsches Afrika Korps (DAK) troops checking their weapons while taking cover in a trench. They maintained their high level of discipline throughout the North African campaign.

at El Alamein was the abundance of mines protecting them. Rommel ordered the planting of more than 45,000 mines between the front line and the rear of the Panzer Army Africa, giving the minefields a somewhat conservative depth of 8 kilometers. German engineers had turned mine laying into an art form, always improving their methods and inventing news types of booby trap.

They laid each mine with a separation of 24 meters between each one, anti-tank and anti-personnel ones in consecutive rows with a typical ratio of 2:1. About 3 percent of the mines were equipped with special traps for the mine-clearing teams. While mine warfare was a military task, many felt a strong aversion to it because of its devious nature that, it was felt, was not compatible with any of the high ideals of chivalrous battle. It was a stab in the back, a murder planned days, or weeks before while the instigator remained unaware of his victim or the damage caused while he remained in no danger. The Germans possessed a number of different mine types to fortify their front at El Alamein. The bounding-type S mine, or "Bouncing Betty" was the size of a beer can and distinguished by three prongs protruding above the ground. When somebody trod on one, there was a small detonation and the main charge was propelled into the air, almost to chest height, where it exploded, spraying 350 steel pellets in all directions to a distance of 150 meters. The anti-tank "Teller" mine was a round metal box, "a little bigger than a plate," according to British sappers, that was buried a little below ground level. It contained 6 kg of explosives that, on detonation, could break a tank track or wreck a truck. Teller mines were often placed one on top of the other, so when the mine-clearing teams defused one and relaxed, they were killed by the second one. This type of mine contributed up to 75 percent of the total of Wehrmacht anti-tank mines during World War II and was so reliable that, even today, Teller mines are still being unearthed in the North African desert in perfect working condition. The Italians had the equivalent in the B4-type mine. It was triangular, and they positioned them with such skill that they did not differ in any respect from their German colleagues. Other mines included the wooden Schu type that was undetectable, as it did not contain any metal parts. Its 200 gms of explosives was sufficient to wound or maim its victim but not kill him. The reasoning behind this mine was that the Germans believed that a soldier cut to pieces, in agony, was a more disheartening sight for his comrades than him being dead. They would also place the detonator some distance in front of the mine, making its detection all the more difficult. In addition, the Germans used more elementary booby traps, based on the simple principle of having the safety pin of a grenade pulled by a trip wire.

General Montgomery talks to 8th Army troops before the decisive Battle of El Alamein. A basic tenet of his command methodology was to make clear down to the last soldier his own role in the forthcoming confrontation.

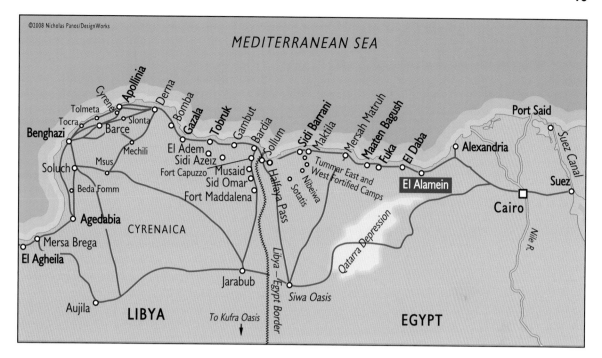

©2008 Nicholas Panos/DesignWorks

There were very few people in the Allied camp who could be considered pessimistic, in spite of the successive misfortunes that had piled up on the "brave 8th Army that had stumbled" (according to Alexander) and the impressive Axis defensive works at El Alamein. General Montgomery (already called "Monty" by his men) needed but a few days to inspire the veterans with a new feeling of self-confidence, a feeling they had not had since Wavell's first sweeping triumph against the Italians during the winter of 1940. Under the inspired leadership of the new commander, who in appearance was "skin and bones," but knew very well what he wanted, the disillusioned troops of the 8th Army quickly realized the first fundamental element of the situation as it now was: There was to be no retreat. Montgomery cancelled all the precautionary plans drawn up by Auchinleck in order to underline his intentions. These plans had anticipated, in the event that Rommel broke through once again, a probable

withdrawal to a new secondary line of defense in the area of the Nile Delta. "This is not a plan," Montgomery growled, annoyed. "By the time our troops withdraw 10 meters, they will have already lost half their fighting spirit."

He made known publicly that he planned to burn the withdrawal plans and, on one occasion, reprimanded a group of Australians who were digging trenches in the rear: "Stop digging there. You won't need them." He gave the order for the trucks that were to help the infantry withdraw to be sent far to the rear, and all tank crews received an express command that looked like a threatening ultimatum: "From now on, the 8th Army shall not surrender an inch to the enemy. Troops shall fight and die at their positions." One of his primary ideas was to create a reserve armored corps, along the lines of the Afrika Korps that would be strengthened by two or three armored divisions.

Montgomery, son of a priest, God-fearing, and an advocate of strict

The long retreat of the 8th Army after its defeat at Gazala and Tobruk in the summer of 1942 only stopped in the El Alamein position, a position offering an ideal defensive line due to the neighboring Qattara Depression to its South. The Axis did not succeed in breaking through this line in July and August and lost the battle of reorganization. (Map design: Nicholas Panos)

Grant tanks had a marked impact on the Allied victory, although operating in the shadow of the more improved M4 Shermans.

discipline, expected his men to obey his orders promptly and without protest. Like many missionaries, he was ostentatious and possessed by an almost messianic wish to convert others to his own principles of war and to prove that his "methodical battle" doctrine was the correct course of action. Montgomery, an unusual character and never an easy colleague, in the context of the British Army, was a strong advocate of centralized command and was the exact opposite of his "democratic" predecessors. Wavell, Ritchie, Auchinleck, even Alexander, were ready to accept the military system they had found without making any kind of revolutionary change. They listened to the advice of their subordinates and left them room for their own initiatives. They commanded more through a system of compromises and improvisations and they were called to face any special situation, as was now about to surface. The British Empire had been governed in this way for centuries, and it was perfectly natural to view this system as ideal.

Montgomery, however, was the other side of the coin. He refused to accept any indication of slack discipline, even in the most

insignificant details, and even staff officers were obligated to show up for lunch on time and with their uniforms tidy.

"An unkempt army is a half-beaten army" he was wont to say. His ideas about military organization related more to the USSR Stahanovites than to the liberal standards of a country with a long parliamentary tradition. A correspondent once said of him: "He believed in surgery and not homoeopathy. If something is wrong or just partly right, then it has to be cut from its roots. If an officer is at fault, he is discharged from his duties on the spot."

At first, his innovations ran into instant or veiled reactions of many officers and even troops who had been used to the vague situation before. A number of jokes began circulating in 8th Army circles, an army known for its caustic humor, about the new strong, absolute commander, like the one about a psychiatrist that was called to Heaven, where Saint Peter told him: "God does not feel well. He thinks he is Montgomery." "Monty" borrowed the traditional public relations tricks used by politicians and started visiting his units wearing the simple black beret of the armored forces (he said the beret's effect "was "was worth two divisions," on the troops' morale) and lost no chance to stressing to his soldiers that their primary mission was to kill as many Germans and Italians they could, saying: "Even priests have to 'clean,' once during week-days and a second time at week-ends." The men who were going to achieve the first decisive Allied victory on land during World War II had mixed feelings of devotion and fear for their leader, characterizing him with the simple but succinct: "Indefatigable during defeat, unbearable during victory."

Alam Halfa

When the general reached North Africa, he was fortunate to discover an experienced 8th Army, forged under real battle conditions. Its three armored divisions (1st, 7th, and 10th) were British, manned by capable and well-trained men. Major-General A. F. Harding's "old faithful 7th" retained its dignified look, obtained through its long experience in the desert, although replacing its aging tanks with the new American type was a priority. Its black-bereted crews were happy being on their own far to the south, where they could maneuver freely in their own daring way, as they never liked the coastal area. The 1st Armoured Division, under Major-General R. Briggs, consisted entirely of veterans and had the asset of its old divisional commander, Lieutenant-General H. Lumsden, as the commanding officer of X Corps. Only one brigade from the 10th, commanded by Major-General A.

H. Gatehouse, had any previous battle experience, while the other two "had not fired a shot in anger from the time of Dunkirk." Another armored division was the 8th, under Major-General C. H. Gairdner, which was another new arrival in the desert. It was equipped with enough Sherman and Grant tanks, but Montgomery decided to attach its brigades to the 10th, leaving just its staff to act out his deception plans.

Two more divisions were British, the 44th and 50th Infantry Divisions. The first was definitely unfortunate, as it had been wandering aimlessly performing secondary duties from the time it had landed in North Africa, without having the chance to prove its worth. The 50th was a veteran division, but as it had suffered such tremendous casualties during the summer, it caused Montgomery to think twice about committing it to the frontline. The empire provided four divisions. While the 1st South African

While many Luftwaffe 88 mm guns were used by Rommel to advance alongside the DAK formations as an anti-tank force, others had to remain in reserve to protect the airfields so that critically needed supplies could be flown in from Italy and Sicily. Here a Flak 18 crew replaces the barrel on its weapon using a Ford 3-tonne truck crane to align the barrel guides with the carriage. The barrel linings had to be replaced periodically, as worn liners affected accuracy. (Bundesarchiv)

A 1936 NSU 501 OSL with a Steib sidecar, requisitioned from private ownership and pressed into Luftwaffe service. Whether the open valve system would last long in the desert sands of North Africa was debatable. (Bundesarchiv)

Division had fought for a while at Gazala, it rarely had the chance to participate in any battle worthy of its reputation since it had arrived in North Africa, following its spectacular and victorious march from Kenya to Addis Ababa. The 2nd New Zealand Division was lucky enough to have survived the Battle of Gazala and had vigorous, experienced warriors in its ranks. The fine 4th Indian Division was still suffering from hard-to-replace casualties from earlier battles, while the 9th Australian Division held the credentials of Tobruk and the early skirmishes at El Alamein. The famous 51st (Highland) Infantry Division was considered the best strike formation in the 8th Army, manned by British "cream of warriors" with exceptionally high morale, eager to exact revenge on the Germans for the ignominy of Saint-Valéry-en-Caux, France, in 1940. Ten splendid divisions were eager for battle and went on taking

revenge on the Germans, who had put them to flight time and time again by the simple expedient of taking advantage of the British high command's errors. What was missing was a capable leader and a clear-cut goal. Montgomery offered the 8th Army both. "Follow me," he said to his troops "and we will crush Rommel." The general believed in himself, so he lost little time in convincing his troops to believe in him. "He walked around the units like a prophet," a journalist wrote, "and his troops loved him. He got them on his side before the battle began. He took care to spread the idea that the 8th Army was an independent strike force, taking commands from no one else but him. He was their commanding officer, and he meant to take them on a personal crusade in Africa."

Troops always admire their commanding general's ability to win the majority of battles, and the 8th

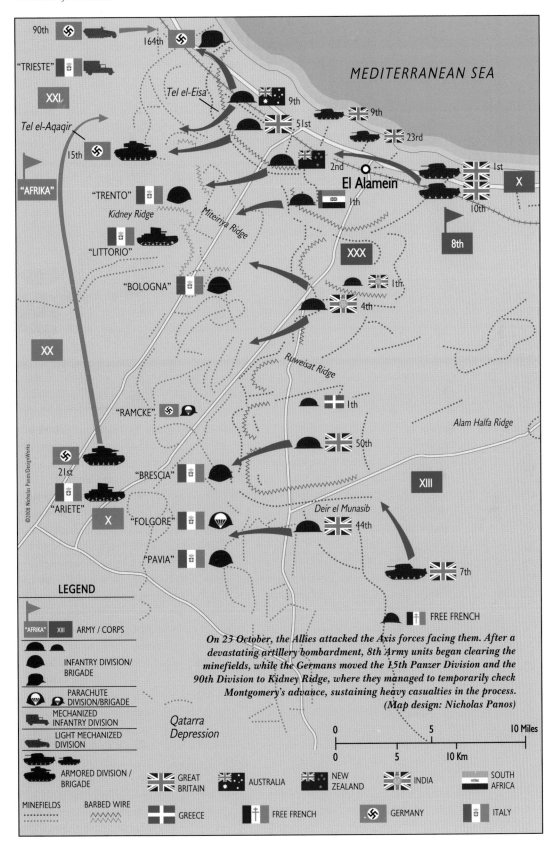

On 23 October, the Allies attacked the Axis forces facing them. After a devastating artillery bombardment, 8th Army units began clearing the minefields, while the Germans moved the 15th Panzer Division and the 90th Division to Kidney Ridge, where they managed to temporarily check Montgomery's advance, sustaining heavy casualties in the process.

(Map design: Nicholas Panos)

Army was in need of solid proof from their new commander that he would actually lead them to victory and was not all talk. The chance was not late in coming. German espionage had received intelligence that a large British convoy, carrying more than 100,000 tons of supplies and equipment was expected to arrive at Suez before the beginning of September, after taking a roundabout route around the Cape of Good Hope. Rommel had to strike before the 8th Army could use that materiel, and the last possible date for the attack had to be scheduled during the next full moon, beginning on 26 August. So, on the night of 30 August 1942. Rommel made his final attempt to break through the 8th Army's front and then push on to Alexandria and the Suez Canal. His plan was essentially a repetition of the tactics that had brought him the impressive victory at Gazala the previous May. Four armored divisions would try to force open the allied lines at the southern end of the front and, after penetrating deep enough to the 8th Army's rear, would then turn north, cutting off communications between all units. To succeed, the operation had to rely on speed, but the British had laid mines in that area to such an extent that the Axis troops wasted the whole of the first night clearing a relatively safe path through the minefields.

Of the 6,000 tons of fuel Rommel had requested, he received just 1,800 tons by the time the panzers were finally ready to take advantage of the paths through the minefields. Rommel was forced to modify his initial plan and reduce the range of his maneuver as he was advancing on the Alam Halfa ridge. Montgomery's predecessors had correctly foreseen such a development, so "Monty" placed 400 tanks, among them many

Grants, in positions that had been already prepared before his arrival in North Africa. Rommels' panzers and other armored vehicles succeeded in destroying many of the new tanks, but while doing so they were mercilessly hammered by the Grants' 75 mm guns and RAF aircraft. By 3 September, Rommel had lost 49 tanks, 3,000 men, and a number of his commanding officers, including Major General (Generalleutnant) Walther K. Nehring of the Afrika Korps, Major General Georg von Bismark of the 21st Panzer Division, and Brigadier General Theodor Graf von Sponeck of the 90th Light Division. He was forced to fall back to his initial positions.

The 8th Army had suffered 1,640 casualties but was aware that it now had a general who could compete with the "Desert Fox" on equal terms. Although, in reality, he reaped the fruits of (Acting) Major-General Eric Dorman-Smith and General Auchinleck's forethought, "wearing" according to historian Correlli Douglas Barnett "a 'second-hand' coat of glory." After the success at Alam Halfa, it was clear that Montgomery had no intention of fighting the Axis forces before being fully prepared in equipment, supplies, and training. This battle would live forever as the famous Battle of El Alamein, outshining all previous battles in the area. His ostensibly slow pace of preparations resulted in heavy criticism from London, with the British prime minister himself taking part in attempts to pressure him into undertaking operations at the soonest possible moment. Once again, in this difficult period of waiting, Montgomery found an ally in Alan Brooke when Brooke wrote, "My next problem will be stopping Churchill from applying pressure on Alexander and Monty to attack before they are

fully ready." Churchill had his own reasons for ardently supporting a great offensive operation by the 8th Army in September: He wanted Great Britain to achieve a decisive victory before the end of autumn, as he also knew that the planned Anglo-American landings in Morocco and Algeria (Operation Torch) would be carried out on 8 November, and it had to be supported by pinning down or destroying the Axis forces at El Alamein. Moreover, the prime minister was looking forward to the prospect of the 8th Army achieving a victory of such magnitude that it would raise the empire's morale and relieve the badly suffering Malta from the suffocating pressure of the Germans, who were using not only Sicilian airfields but also those in North Africa.

Montgomery, meanwhile, was determined not to attack before October, when he estimated that the necessary land and air forces would have been assembled and his new reserves would have been acclimatized to the exacting desert conditions. In fact, he did not hesitate to warn

Churchill that, if he insisted on the operation starting in September, he would have to find another commander to carry it out. "It was blackmail," Montgomery later admitted, but it paid off, and the voices for an early attack fell silent.

The 8th Army commander had serious reasons to be cautious in engaging his forces in a new battle without adequate preparation. This huge force was not yet ready to engage in a decisive confrontation, although it had two years' experience fighting on this particular front. Enough fresh officers and men had recently reinforced the army, but Montgomery found they lacked proper training. The British general, having established as one of his goals the vast improvement in the physical condition and fighting skills of his men after the end of the Battle of Alam Halfa, began sending complete units to the rear, at different times, in order to train them in the theory and practice of war in the desert and hone them with large exercises carried out on terrain similar to the El Alamein line. Conscripts practised firing 6-pdr anti-tank guns

Many Ausf F, G, and H saw service in North Africa. This Ausf H is seen passing a destroyed British Matilda infantry support tank. The Matilda was more heavily armored than the PzKpfw III Ausf F, G or H, although it was slower and mechanically unreliable. (National Archives)

The crew of a German self-propelled anti-tank gun hunts for targets on a chilly desert morning. It is equipped with a Czech-made 47 mm gun mounted on an old Panzer I chassis, a powerful combination in the early years of the war.

against moving targets on six specially constructed firing ranges near the coast, while groups of troops from 56 different engineer units trained in the most advanced techniques of mine-lifting at the 8th Army's Minefield Clearance School. Special care was shown by the general in the formation of X Corps, which he assigned to Lieutenant-General H. Lumsden. This corps exchanged its signals services with that of XXX Corps, since the latter was better equipped for a mobile war. The 51st (Highland) Infantry Division was reassembled, as its brigades had been scattered across the army, fulfilling various minor tasks, and the 44th Infantry Division relieved the New Zealanders in the frontline, with the Kiwis being pulled back to rest and train in a quiet coastal area by Burg el Arab. The 1st and 7th Armoured Divisions also exchanged with an armored brigade taking up position between themselves and the 1st Fighting French Brigade Group under General Marie Pierre Koenig, taking charge of the front's southernmost extremity, as they had done at Gazala.

Careful preparation

Montgomery took very little time to make his decisions, as far as the operational part was concerned. His plan was for an attack against the front's most fortified northern sector. In order to achieve total surprise, under the watchful eyes of Lieutenant-Colonel Charles Richardson, he set in motion the most complicated, elaborate and masterly plan for the concealment of his forces and the deception of the enemy ever put in practice by the British Army. The goal was to persuade the Germans that the British intended to attack in the south, so they would scatter their mobile reserves and remove more infantry forces from the point where the actual allied attack would materialize. The

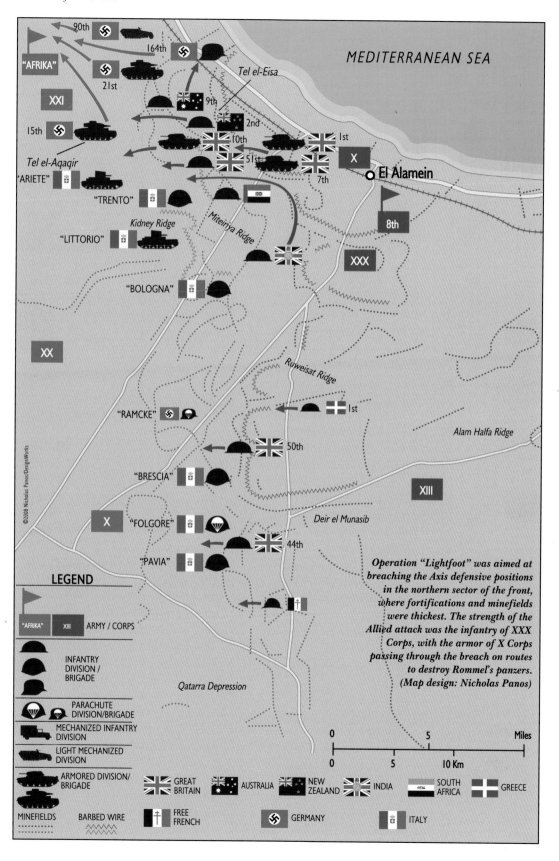

MEDITERRANEAN SEA

90th

164th

"AFRIKA"

21st

XXI

15th

Tel el-Aqaqir

"ARIETE"

Tel el-Eisa

9th

2nd

10th

51st

7th

1st

X

El Alamein

8th

"TRENTO"

Kidney Ridge

"LITTORIO"

Miteirya Ridge

XXX

"BOLOGNA"

XX

Ruweisat Ridge

"RAMCKE"

1st

Alam Halfa Ridge

50th

"BRESCIA"

XIII

X

"FOLGORE"

Deir el Munasib

"PAVIA"

44th

Qatarra Depression

Operation "Lightfoot" was aimed at breaching the Axis defensive positions in the northern sector of the front, where fortifications and minefields were thickest. The strength of the Allied attack was the infantry of XXX Corps, with the armor of X Corps passing through the breach on routes to destroy Rommel's panzers.
(Map design: Nicholas Panos)

©2008 Nicholas Panos/DesignWorks

0   5   Miles

0   5   10 Km

LEGEND

"AFRIKA"   XIII   ARMY / CORPS

INFANTRY DIVISION / BRIGADE

PARACHUTE DIVISION/BRIGADE

MECHANIZED INFANTRY DIVISION

LIGHT MECHANIZED DIVISION

ARMORED DIVISION/ BRIGADE

MINEFIELDS   BARBED WIRE

GREAT BRITAIN   AUSTRALIA   NEW ZEALAND   INDIA   SOUTH AFRICA   GREECE

FREE FRENCH   GERMANY   ITALY

A Pzkpfw III leads an armored column. This vehicle was armed with the 37 mm gun, which was the armament that the Mk III began the war with.

speed of the construction of the pipeline extension was calculated to allay the Germans' fears of an immediate attack, at least, until the British had completed this "vital" supply artery to provide drinking water. In contrast, all aerial photos Rommel received from the northern sector revealed a dominance of general inactivity. The British, meanwhile, worked unceasingly under cover of darkness, transporting 3,000 tons of ammunition to the El Imayid railroad station while concealing 2,000 tons of fuel in 100 ditches around the El Alamein railroad station. Food was carefully stockpiled and vehicles carefully covered with camouflage nets. On the eve of the battle, when the tanks moved to their jumping-off points disguised as trucks with removable covers, Richardson took care to immediately replace them with 400 dummy trucks in their original parking place, so their absence would go unnoticed. The infantry occupied its planned positions, moving forward only at night and, according to Cartier, "soldiers spent their days packed in their narrow trenches, under clouds of flies, forbidden to move for any reason." The 8th Armoured Division (a "phantom" division) carried on with its usual signals traffic even when X Corps left its exercise area. All the 8th Army call signs and frequencies were frequently changed and there were also long periods of radio silence so the enemy would not suspect anything about the time of the real attack.

Montgomery had chosen the night of 23 October to launch his attack, taking into consideration that Rommel's forces were being reinforced with 20 to 25 tanks a week, while intelligence had also been received that the German 22nd Infantry Division was to be sent to Africa at the

enemy closely scrutinized the 8th Army, trying to guess its intentions through aerial photography, studying newly built or improved roads, changes in the volume of vehicle traffic, changes in the size and number of matériel depots, and improvements in water pipelines. At the same time, it was collecting intelligence by changes in the density of signal traffic, from its agents in the Delta area or from the interrogation of prisoners of war. The British, however, managed to "get their enemy off to sleep" by supplying him with false intelligence and diligently disguising reality.

Three fully equipped "phantom" heavy artillery regiments were formed, with bogus equipment and crews constructed from plywood and cloth to make Luftwaffe photo reconnaissance believe that Montgomery had concentrated strong forces on his southern sector in order to attack along the edge of the Qattara Depression. A 30-kilometer bogus water pipeline, with many dummy pumping stations and fake water reservoirs along its length, was laid southwards down to Samaket Gaballa, where the desert was dotted with at least 700 intentionally badly camouflaged supply dumps. The

beginning of November. Training the 8th Army's troops would be completed by 23 October, and the full moon would help the mine-clearing teams in their hazardous duties so paths would be opened through the giant minefields protecting the Axis defensive positions. These teams would have just eight hours until dawn to lift enough mines for the infantry and tanks to safely cross, while the full moon period would provide acceptable conditions to complete the operation for the week after.

As zero hour approached, the 8th Army could count on a particularly satisfactory 2:1 superiority over the Axis forces in almost every aspect. Its troops numbered 195,000 against 104,000 Germans and Italians, operational tanks 1,029 against Rommel's 496. The qualitative difference was overwhelming. Many of the British tanks were heavier even than the PzKpfw IVs, while the 300

Italian armored vehicles could not be considered a worthy opponent. The 8th Army was very well supplied, which was in direct contrast to Panzer Army Africa that still suffered from the same dire shortages that had deprived it, to a great extent, of victory in the summer of 1942. Montgomery's tank strength increased from 896 to 1,354 (although many of them were in the repair shops at the time) in five and a half weeks, from the end of the Battle of Alam Halfa to the beginning of the Battle of El Alamein. These included 285 Shermans, 246 Grants, 421 Crusaders, 167 Stuarts, 223 Valentines, 6 Matildas, and 6 Churchills (the last on field trials.) The 2-pdr guns increased from 450 to 550 and 6-pdrs from 400 to 850, while field guns increased from 216 to 832. The Panzer Army Africa was in for a great technical surprise.

Panzer Army Africa contemplated the next round of operations with great caution and desperation,

A PzKpfw III Ausf J of 15th Panzer Division Deutsches Afrikakorps (DAK) was brush-painted with camouflage to hide it from patrolling aircraft. It carries the division pennant on the radio antenna. The vehicle was painted overall brown, with the turret number red outlined white, and the name "BESTIE" in black.

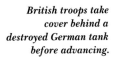

British troops take cover behind a destroyed German tank before advancing.

marked by the absence of its forceful commander. This was in direct contrast to the atmosphere of rejuvenated trust and power prevalent in the 8th Army. The charismatic Rommel, who had led them to such amazing victories, was forced to leave on 23 September for Semmering, in Austria, to restore his health that had been undermined by the hardships of the strenuous summer campaign. The 51-year-old field marshal despite his indomitable vigor, was now paying the price of excessive fatigue, having driven his physical condition to the limits of exhaustion. In addition to the chronic gastric and intestinal problems he already had, he now also suffered from a dysfunctional circulatory system and nasal diphtheria. With the "Desert Fox" 2,000 kilometers away, command of Panzer Army Africa was given to Lieutenant-General (General der Kavallerie) Georg Stumme, a 56-years-old, robust Eastern Front veteran who had commanded a corps but unfortunately also suffered from high blood pressure. As if past misfortunes were not sufficient, during September the Panzer Army Africa Staff was decimated by various illnesses with its chief of staff,

Brigadier General Fritz Gause suffering from severe headaches, Colonel (Oberst i.G.) Siegfried Westphal hospitalized with jaundice, and Major (Major i.G.) F.W. von Mellenthin bedridden by amoebic dysentery. Fortunately, the Germans had capable officers as formation commanding generals. Lieutenant General (General der Panzertruppe) Wilhelm Ritter von Thoma of the Afrika Korps, Brigadier General Heinz von Randow of the 21st Panzer Division, Brigadier Generals Ulrich Kleemann (until 31 October) and Theodor Graf von Sponeck of the 90th Light Division, Brigadier General Gustav von Vaerst of the 15th Panzer Division and Colonel Carl Hans Lungershausen of the 164th Infantry Division. Stumme made his own particular contribution to the Battle of El Alamein's outcome by making an error that Rommel would never commit. He divided his forces equally along the front, while preferring to place his panzer divisions in static positions, instead of maintaining them in a high state of readiness for use for counterattacks.

No one in the Allied camp claimed that the Battle of El Alamein would be easy for the 8th Army, in spite of indications to the contrary. Montgomery was not a man to fall into the classic error of underestimating his opponent, as was shown by the plan of operation, "Lightfoot," he had prepared. Under cover of a heavy artillery barrage, four infantry divisions from Lieutenant-General Sir Oliver Leese's XXX Corps (1st South African, 9th Australian, 2nd New Zealand, and 51st Highland) would move at night through the minefields, neutralizing enemy machine gun pits and trenches. When they had overcome the enemy defenses and the mine-clearing teams had cleared safe paths, the time would arrive for pushing forward the tanks of X Corps (1st and 10th Armoured Divisions positioned at Wadi Natrun, the same distance as between El Alamein and Cairo). They would pass through the infantry lines to lure the Axis armor into battle and eliminate it. Another attack by Lieutenant-General B. G. Horrocks' XIII Corps would begin later to the south. Its mission was to pin down the enemy reserves and continue to present Stumme with the dilemma of where exactly the main Allied effort was to fall. In the meantime, RAF aircraft would continue to bomb enemy positions and airfields deep in the rear, endeavoring to stop any intervention by the German and Italian Air Forces.

On the night of 23 October, all was ready, with Montgomery not neglecting the smallest detail. At least 2,000 military policemen, equipped with white gloves and red caps, would take care of traffic regulation, enabling the armored columns to drive toward the expected breaches in the enemy defenses along six parallel routes of advance. Military medical personnel checked on blood and plasma bottles in special refrigerated trucks, and the mine-clearing teams were fully prepared to carry out their mission, equipped with 500 mine detectors, 88,000 lamps to light the cleared paths at night, and a further 180 kilometers of tape to mark the cleared lanes for the infantry.

Montgomery retired early that night. On his wall hung Rommel's portrait with, next to it, an excerpt from Shakespeare's Henry V: "O God of battles! Steel my soldiers' hearts!" Lieutenant-General Sir Leslie Morshead, commanding officer of the 9th Australian Division, wrote: "We are anticipating a tough battle that will last, no doubt, many days. We do not delude ourselves. I'm sure we will win and end all this coming and going in the desert."

Eight kilometers away, Stumme did not have the slightest idea about

A German PzKpfw IV in North Africa.

Two PzKpfw III Ausf Ls in Libya in 1942. Both are overall brown, and no markings are visible.

the strength of the blow that was about to fall on his forces. Montgomery's deceptive ruses had persuaded the Germans that any future attack would be carried out in the south no earlier than the beginning of November. This impression gave Stumme a false sense of security allied to one of profound relief, as he knew he lacked the quantities of fuel needed to allow the panzers to maneuver quickly along the front's 60 kilometers in reaction to any enemy attempts to penetrate it. The general felt bitter about the whole situation that could lead to a disaster and often reported to Berlin and Rome that the Panzer Army barely managed to survive: "We dig a pit in order to fill another one. So it is impossible to create reserves that will allow us to face all kinds of different situations and have freedom of movement, something literally vital for the Army." On 11 September, he had tried to obtain a promise of a further 35,000 tons of supplies that, in addition to the 30,000 tons promised by the Italians for September (but not yet received!), would give him a reserve of eight units of firepower and 30 units of fuel (one unit represented the amount of supplies the Army required for a full day of action). In answer to the 11,000 troop

replacements he requested, he only received the young paratroopers of the Ramcke Brigade that had arrived by air from Crete "without any preparation and without having their endurance tested, in the month of August in such a burning climate," as German correspondents noted. Consequently, 12 percent of the paratroopers, aged 17 to 20 years old, were always hospitalized by various illnesses and heat stroke, which also happened with the 164th Light Division that took up positions along the northern sector of the front. German experts commented, "Wehrmacht High Command (OKW) could not see that the Afrika Korps had managed to balance its lack in material and personnel until then by the value of its leadership and the heroism of its troops. The situation had drastically changed. The Panzer Army was no longer fighting in the vast desert. It was, now, trapped between the Qattara Depression and the sea, in a particularly difficult condition." Stumme's troops had to deal with food shortages, and hepatitis and dysentery cases were multiplying. The Panzer Army received only half the fuel it requested, and each panzer division could barely rely on 100 battle-worthy tanks.

"Lightfoot" over mines

The deep drone of RAF aircraft was heard at 21:30 over the lines of El Alamein on their way to strike targets at the enemy rear. Ten minutes later, the order "open fire!" echoed in the cold desert night, and the silence was shattered by the deafening thunder of the 8th Army's 908 guns opening fire across the front. This 20-minute barrage, which could only be compared to the annihilating storms of steel of World War I, threw an unprecedented number of shells over German and Italian positions. Explosions could be heard from as far as Alexandria, 100 kilometers away. The British gunners soon lost their hearing from the thunder of their guns, and their thick gloves began wearing out due to the heating up of the gun barrels. A New Zealand officer wrote that he felt the earth dancing under his feet "like a drum's membrane." Over half of Montgomery's guns were over 105 mm caliber, and the rolling barrage they laid moved forward 100 meters every five minutes, in accordance with the methods typical of 1916. German and Italian batteries had been silent to conserve ammunition for the next phase of the battle, while each Allied gun fired around 300 shells. Even if the Axis had the ammunition, they could have done no better as, mostly, they were equipped with inadequate and obsolete Italian field guns with a range of just 7 kilometers. Almost 70,000 men and 600 tanks of the 8th Army took part in the attack's first phase, concentrating their forces on the boundary between the Italian "Trento" Division and the German 164th Light Infantry Division.

The intensity of fire was such that it created indescribable confusion in

Major General Schmidt, commander of the Bardia group, tours the front lines to assess the situation and prepare his strategy. (Bundesarchiv)

the Axis lines. As the shells burst, whole acres of minefields were exploding, scattering sky-high fountains of earth and shrapnel, and pulverizing the barbed wire. Shelters were crushed and trenches collapsed under the murderous deluge of 900 shells per minute. There were many cases of German and Italian soldiers killed by concussion, with their bodies later discovered without any visible wounds.

Stumme was to be no exception to the atmosphere of surprise and desperation that existed everywhere. His signals network was destroyed within seconds by the artillery onslaught, and the German general was cut off from all his divisions and regiments. He decided to go to the front in the morning, escorted by one of his staff officers (the intelligence officer Colonel Büchting) with Corporal Wolf as his driver, to try to re-establish contact with his units and get a better overall picture of the situation. He refused to be accompanied by an escort and a radio-equipped vehicle because, he said, he was only going to the 90th Light Division area. Eventually Stumme's car, jerked about by nearby shell bursts, entered a field of fire of Australian machine guns and Büchting was mortally wounded in the head and fell forward onto the windscreen. Wolf tried to reverse out

General Cruwell, later to be appointed commander of the Afrika Korps, congratulates Oberst Michel who had escaped from the British after three days in captivity. (Bundesarchiv)

of the field of fire but, in his panic, he did not realize that Stumme had leapt out of the car to protect himself from the machine gun fire. However, the shock had brought about a heart attack and Stumme dropped dead. Meanwhile, his driver, without realizing what had happened, drove off. The Axis forces now found themselves without a commander, albeit temporarily, and the battle was not yet 24 hours old. It would take two days to find the corpse of the unfortunate General Stumme and, in the meantime, overall command fell on Major General Wilhelm Ritter von Thoma, commanding officer Afrika Korps, who had little experience of North African conditions.

Montgomery's infantry began moving forward immediately after the artillery opened fire. Captain Murray, who was observing it, described the unforgettable sight, "Successive lines of figures with helmets, rifles in hand and bayonets shining in the moonlight but, above all, the sound of bagpipes. As they passed in front of us, they gave us the "thumbs up' sign, and we

continued watching them as they advanced towards the enemy lines that were shrouded in smoke. The enemy received them with heavy fire." The infantry advanced in the manner in which they had been trained, at a steady pace of 50 meters a minute with a separation of three meters between each man. Each member of the 51st (Highland) Division in the northern sector carried his personal haversack, two hand grenades, 50 rifle rounds, rations for one day, a water canteen, his personal entrenching tool, and four empty, folded sandbags that were to be used as cover from shells bursting overhead after, of course, being filled with sand. White Saint Andrew crosses, made of thin cloth, were attached to the back of the small knapsacks to help the men orientate themselves and not lose contact with their column in the darkness.

Mine-clearing teams started their death-defying duty as soon as they reached the barbed wire marking the boundaries of the German and Italian minefields. It was practically impossible to lift the minefields in their entirety, although by then the artillery barrage had already exploded many of the mines. Montgomery's sappers set out to clear 8-meter-wide paths that would allow tanks to cross the minefields in line astern. Anti-tank mines were defused by removing their detonators, and the deadly S-mine by inserting nails in the small holes that had contained the safety pins before being laid. After clearing, each lane was marked with white tape and orange or green lamps showing where the infantry and tanks could move freely. Those courageous mine-clearing teams managed to clear lanes, at a rate of 200 meters an hour, using mine detectors that could detect buried metal objects by producing a high-pitched whistle through the operators' headphones. In spite of their dedication and skill, these men paid a heavy price for their success before the morning of 24 October dawned. Hundreds of booby traps exploded, killing many troops. An officer in charge of one of these teams had to change three different vehicles after each had been destroyed by a mine, while many of his colleagues were not so lucky and were blown to pieces by S and Teller mines. In one case, an Allied 113-kilogram bomb had been skillfully buried by the Germans, and it decimated a 30-man platoon in a fraction of a second. Mines killed seven engineer officers of a Black Watch battalion before first light. One British company tried to traverse a minefield but suddenly found itself in another that was covered by enemy fire and was wiped out.

The Allies, however, were stubborn and persistent, imbued with the discipline Montgomery had enforced. Infantrymen advanced at a snail's pace, gradually discovering the surreal horror their artillery shells had caused in the Italo-German lines: a dead German signals officer with the telephone receiver still in his ear, another holding a cigarette in one hand and matches in the other, body parts scattered widely across large areas, and blood still running from the closed doors of an ambulance. Alarich Jacob, the war correspondent, who ventured to visit an Australian advanced field hospital, could stand there but a few minutes: "In one of the tents, a doctor was amputating a hand, men were bleeding profusely in another while they were being continuously transfused. The doctors were working like over-employed butchers on a Saturday night."

The advance was slowed down even further by a lack of mine detectors. Some proved defective, while others were destroyed in the battle, resulting in the sappers having to prod the earth with their bayonets. So the rate of advance turned into that of a man on his knees desperately groping in the sand. This development created justified concern across all sectors of the front. Could the Allies open enough paths and defuse enough mines for the waiting armored forces to secure a 16-by-8-kilometer pocket by morning? This task seemed impossible during the night of 23 October 1942. Montgomery's troops crawled through the minefields under the deadly fire of enemy machine guns; surprisingly the majority of them had not been hit by the artillery barrage. Adding to the dust, smoke, mines, and general confusion on the battlefield was the fact that two divisions from two different corps were trying to clear lanes through the minefields and move their vehicles into the same confined area from which the enemy had not been completely driven out.

Rommel briefs his staff prior to the summer 1942 offensive. (Bundesarchiv)

"A chaotic situation reined," a British officer admitted, "resulting in no one knowing where he was or where friend and foe were." Eighth Army tanks were not yet on the move in the northern sector, but their engines were running, and they were behind the infantry who desperately trying to open the way. In spite of the magnificent fighting spirit shown by Montgomery's troops, it was impossible to keep to the initial time schedule.

The sappers had not completed their mission task even by the morning of 24 October, with only the 9th Australian Division and the 2nd New Zealand Division (from the five assault divisions in the north) showing any notable progress, crossing the minefields and seizing positions on Hill 28 and Miteiriya Ridge, respectively. The South Africans had also achieved some minor success but at a price of 350 casualties. In the south, the secondary thrust of XIII Corps, aimed at pinning down enough enemy reserves, achieved but scant results, and the Free French were unable to consolidate their positions west of Qaret El Himeimat. However, the Germans were slow to respond, with Von Thoma proving indecisive and unable to promptly ascertain which of the Allied attacking thrusts was the main one, so he hesitated to concentrate his reserves in any specific sector. The 21st Panzer Division and "Ariete" Armored Division remained in their positions in the south, while the 90th Light Division and "Trieste" Mechanized Division remained where they were near the coast in the El Daba area. He only used the 15th Panzer and "Littorio" Armored Divisions to cover the breach in his lines by attacking toward Hill 28 where danger appeared imminent.

While 8th Army mine-clearing teams continued crawling forward inch by inch, X Corps armor, which had to advance across three paths with a distance of 500 meters between them, was still jammed, powerless at its start lines, in spite of the fact that it had absolute priority on all paths after 0200. Every minefield was covered in dust, there were masses of vehicles everywhere, and the sappers' markings were difficult to distinguish. As the tanks and other vehicles slowly crawled through hanging clouds of dust, their engines began overheating. Montgomery began to doubt the fighting spirit of the "black berets," noting that the "X Corps commanding officer did not show the required strength and determination when the going got tough." So he ordered the tanks to move, regardless of the fact that some paths had not been cleared.

Armored unit commanders were upset at this order, expecting their tanks to sustain heavy casualties, not only from mines but also from the enemy anti-tank guns that lay in ambush, neither of which had yet been cleared by the infantry. Lieutenant-General H. Lumsden showed his obvious annoyance with Montgomery's decision, arguing that in order for the armor to win, you first had to know how to control it, and "if one has no patience to use armor at the most opportune moment, a mass slaughter will occur. It is not a task for armor to engage guns." Lumsden suggested that X Corps should fall back to regroup west of Miteiriya Ridge, to be thrown into battle when the sappers had completed their task.

Montgomery, later, called the night of 24-25 October as "the real battle crisis." Panzer Army Africa began reacting decisively and with urgency, a fact causing the British to infer, correctly, that Rommel had returned to the front. Still, in compliance with

Montgomery's orders, the tanks began moving forward under cover of darkness, but were extremely unlucky. Around 2200, bombs dropped by a Luftwaffe aircraft hit many of the Sherwood Foresters' (Nottinghamshire and Derbyshire Regiment) supply vehicles and, as they were jammed together, they were set on fire one after the other with 25 being destroyed in a very short time. Flames leaping from the condemned vehicles and the flashes of explosions turned the night into day, helping the defenders to concentrate their fire on the British tanks, resulting in a terrible massacre. The Staffordshire Yeomanry's (Queen's Own Royal Regiment) vehicles were hit by fire from German 88 mm anti-aircraft guns, and Major John Lakin watched as 27 tanks were "set on fire, one by one, like birthday cake candles." Lumsden sent an urgent message to Montgomery's staff, asking him to immediately suspend the attack when he realized the extent of the disaster. "Monty's" chief of staff, Brigadier Freddie de Guingand, who received the message, acted at once and, although it was known that Montgomery hated being woken up at night, called the X and XXX Corps commanders for a meeting with the commanding officer 8th Army during the first hours after midnight.

The 1942 "dead tired" corps chiefs reached Montgomery's armored command vehicle at 0330 on 25 October. Cartier later wrote, "and Montgomery, displeased that he had to get out of bed, welcomed them like they were dogs." He listened to Lumsden as he set out his views without interrupting him and clearly showed him that he completely disagreed with what he said. The commanding officer X Corps suggested suspending the attack and immediately withdrawing the tanks.

A captured CMP 6pdr Portee is inspected by DAK personnel. The British 6pdr (57mm) was an excellent light-medium anti-tank gun that was eventually used as the basis for the US 57mm M1 AT gun. This crew has apparently already settled down next to the truck with a sunshade and blanket "mattress." (Bundesarchiv)

Obsolete tanks were often utilized as fixed bunkers. This Cruiser Mark IV has been dug-in on the Libya-Egypt border and is crewed by Italians. This photo clearly shows that the shape of the turret on the Mark IV was the result of attaching additional armor plates. (Bundesarchiv)

Lumsden further warned that British armor would come face-to-face with numerous Axis guns after Miteiriya Ridge, which would be equally catastrophic, as experience gained in the desert had shown. He also suggested that the 8th Army commander talk directly to Gatehouse, which Montgomery did, reproaching the 10th Armoured Division commander for being 16 kilometers behind the forward line. Montgomery bluntly declared that the plan had to be followed to the end. Any thought of withdrawal was unacceptable and, if Lumsden and his subordinates were in no mood to push their forces forward, others would be found to continue the advance. With this rigid attitude, Montgomery showed his commanders, in essence, a method of war unknown to them until then, a method reminiscent of the stubborn mass attacks of World War I. The 8th Army commander calculated, with clinical logic, that he still possessed at least 900 tanks and the armor he had lost so far was expendable. On the other hand, his infantry reserves were limited, and the first 30 hours of the El Alamein battle had cost him over 6,000 casualties.

The Panzer Army was now once more under Field Marshal Rommel's command, as he had been ordered to return to Africa by an extremely anxious Hitler who, as yet, was unaware of the reason behind Stumme's disappearance, although Rommel was equally aware that "there were no more laurels to be reaped in Africa." After reaching Panzer Army headquarters a little before sunset, Rommel listened to Lieutenant General von Thoma's unedifying report. Fuel shortages were most acute, with the Panzer Army barely having enough fuel for three days of action, so every major move would be extremely difficult to execute. Rommel, who had always been mistrustful of the Wehrmacht High Command (OKW) but trusting of Hitler, at last clearly realized the emptiness of the Fuhrer's promises. Just a month earlier, during discussions at the Fuhrer's headquarters at Rastenburg in Eastern Prussia, Hitler spoke to him reassuringly, "Do not worry, we will capture Alexandria without fail." He talked, in a typical outburst of megalomania and military fantasy, about the special ferries without keels that would carry supplies to Africa and solve the supply problems, about the Nebelwerfer rocket launcher brigade that would be sent to Africa, even about the 40 Tiger heavy tanks that would follow straight after rolling out off the production lines.

Reality, however, was far removed from the optimistic picture painted by the delusional leader at Rastenburg. Rommel's fuel and ammunition supplies were dangerously low, and the promised new weapons had not arrived by October. The Battle of El Alamein had taken the form of a war of attrition that the Germans could not hope to win. Panzer Army Africa troops fought viciously for each and every rocky outcrop, each hole in the ground, and every meter of barbed

wire, "Rivers of blood had been shed on wretched pieces of land for which, under other circumstances, even the poorest Arab would not give a pfennig," Rommel later admitted. The Axis knew how vital it was to repulse the blow the 8th Army was trying to strike at El Alamein and had managed to prevent a breakthrough during the first crucial hours. Montgomery, meanwhile, engaged and wore down Rommel's forces one by one. The 15th Panzer Division, which was on the receiving end of the main blow on Kidney Ridge (Hill 28), had just 31 operational tanks from the 119 it had initially fielded. Rommel knew that his only remaining hope was to get away from the type of war Montgomery was imposing on the Germans and attempt to avoid the overwhelming enemy artillery, which was firing 500 shells for each one from his guns. He had to find space to maneuver, to once again fight a war of movement on the battlefield. He believed that, compared to the enemy, he was superior in this type of warfare, and the German troops and his skills would more than compensate for their numerical inferiority. The Panzer Army,

however, had to ration every drop of its available fuel, and move conservatively, which would not allow any overindulgence in spectacular maneuvers. Rommel was eagerly waiting for the arrival of the Italian tanker "Proserpina" at Tobruk that would unload 7,000 tons of fuel, but the ship ended up at the bottom of the Mediterranean, struck by a British aerial torpedo, with the tanker "Luisiano" following it two days later, also the result of torpedoes. In consequence, the Panzer Army was forced, undeniably, to follow Montgomery's pace and accept the war of attrition. Rommel tried desperately to regain his old front line, but failed. The ferocity of the British defenses on Kidney Ridge, the intensity of the artillery fire, and the unremitting air attacks by RAF fighters worried him about the outcome of the 15th Panzer Division's counterattacks there. German and Italian morale began to waver, and the field marshal felt the pressure increasing on him and his army with each hour. "A very tough struggle," he wrote to his wife on 27 October. "No one can feel the burden I have shouldered."

British trucks, like this 1/2 ton Canadian Dodge 4x4 radio truck, generally had very good desert performance and were highly prized by the DAK. This vehicle retains its British tan paint scheme, very recently applied by the look of the painted tires. For recognition purposes, the new owners have added a crude cross. (Bundesarchiv)

Armored "Supercharge"

Montgomery certainly must have been especially worried, although he was reluctant to publicly admit that he harbored the slightest doubt about the success of his plan. His goal was to achieve a cataclysmic victory over Rommel, but until 26 October (the third day of the battle) most allied forces were still far from capturing the objectives they had been assigned for the first eight hours of the operation. In addition, they had suffered heavy casualties and captured just 1,400 Italians and 600 Germans. "Monty" realized that, unless a new attack was launched to overcome this stalemate, his units might possibly lose their impetus and, more important, their will to win. The general spent most of the day isolated in his command vehicle and, when he finally emerged, had a new plan.

"The plan had the simplicity of genius," wrote Lieutenant-Colonel

This captured British Canadian CMP truck has been converted into a self-propelled mount for a 20 mm Flak 30. The vehicle has been repainted in overall yellow/brown. The flag was displayed as an identification aid for Luftwaffe pilots. (Bundesarchiv)

Weart, an intelligence officer on Montgomery's staff. The greatest Allied progress until that moment had been accomplished in the north where the indomitable 9th Australian Division had penetrated the enemy's minefield and was moving northeast toward the coast, creating a pocket that became known by the shape of the hill dominating the area, the "Thumb." The Australians had a good field of observation over the coastal road and the railroad line and were now threatening two German regiments, which they had bypassed on their southern side. Montgomery felt that a pincer strike in the Australian sector would, in all probability, lead to the seizing of the road and, in consequence, the cutting of Rommel's supplies. The New Zealanders, who were to be the spearhead of the new operation, were pulled back for a short rest and regrouping. XIII Corps would, temporarily, undertake defensive operations, and its 7th Armoured

Division, which had done so well with its southern diversionary operation in the south, would be attached to X Corps as the corps reserve.

The Australians, meanwhile, were extremely exposed on the "Thumb" but were under strict orders to dig in and stay put to help Montgomery's general plan. Naturally, Rommel had not forgotten the ground they had gained and immediately sent the 90th Light Division and the 21st Panzer Division to the area under threat. It was a risky decision, as the "Fox" was well aware that the low fuel reserves would not allow the reassignment of these armored units to the south again if a new crisis broke out there. However, Rommel did not have the luxury of long-term operational planning. He had to react directly to any existing danger with the hope that he would not have to face a new threat from another direction. The Germans launched strong counter-attacks against the Australians throughout 30 and 31 October by pushing in three battle-worthy mobile divisions astride the coastal road, but with little success. Von Thoma and his chief of staff, Major General Fritz Bayerlein, in the Afrika Korps headquarters, came to the conclusion that it was best to withdraw the 125th Motorised Infantry Regiment (Panzergrenadier-Regiment (mot) 125) from Thompson's Post, where the Australians were closing in, and resign themselves to the loss of the regiment's heavy weapons, rather than sacrifice the whole regiment. But Rommel disagreed and ordered the counter-attacks to continue on 1 November. This was to turn out to be an unfortunate decision, which would give decisive advantages to Montgomery.

Churchill, in London, was deeply worried. Fearing that Montgomery,

when he relieved the New Zealanders for a much-needed rest, was giving up the attack, he asked Alan Brooke sharply, "What is your Montgomery doing right now by letting the battle fade away?" In reality, the 8th Army commander was "toughening up" his war plan. He had decided, after being informed that Rommel was moving his elite mobile reserves to the north, to move the weight of his attack 8 kilometers to the south of the area the Australians were contesting, issuing orders for them to continue the battle to enlarge the gap they had created in order to maintain the enemy's attention. The great thrust, code named "Supercharge," would fall in a sector that was the boundary between the German and Italian forces. Its first objective was a 6-kilometer penetration, and the destruction of a threatening concentration of Axis guns on the Sidi Abd el Rahman track. XXX Corps would undertake the

Regrettably only a partial view, this photo of a PzKpfw III stowage bin shows most of the markings carried by tanks of the PzRgt 8, 15th Panzer Division. The "1" is black and white, the palm tree white, and the 15. Panzer Division sign and PzRgt 8 emblem (a wolfsangel) are in red. (Bundesarchiv)

attack, with the experienced 2nd New Zealand Division as its spearhead. This division was under the command of Lieutenant-General Sir Bernard Freyberg, V.C., a veteran of the World War I Gallipoli campaign and the battles of the Somme, and, more recently, the ones on continental Greece and Crete. The New Zealanders would attack, supported by two more British brigades, the151st (50th (Northumbrian) Infantry Division) and 152nd (51st (Highland) Infantry Division), following a renewed, intense artillery barrage. They would advance a distance of 2,000 meters from the Rahman track, halt, and then the 9th Australian Division and the 1st Armoured Division would cross between them to break the Axis guns and extend the breach. Montgomery hoped that this move, more methodically and meticulously timed than that of 23 October, would finally lead to the destruction of Rommel's Panzer Army when X Corps would consolidate its positions in the Tell el Aqqaqir area and face, in a great tank battle, the remaining panzers.

Operation "Supercharge," was "a slow military ballet, reminding us of a precision peacetime exercise," Cartier commented. It was to exceed any other confrontation the 8th Army troops had been through until then, both in terms of ferocity and death. At a meeting before the battle, Brigadier J.C. Currie, 9th Armoured Brigade's commanding officer, noted that this mission would, in all probability, result in his command sustaining up to 50 percent casualties, to which Freyberg responded that "(the army commander) was aware of the risk and has accepted the possibility of losing 100 percent casualties."

At 0100 on 2 November 1942, 360 guns repeated their barrage against the Axis minefields west of the Miteiriya Ridge, once again turning the cold desert night into day and unleashing 15,000 shells to create hell in the German lines. This storm of fire advanced at the steady rate of 100 meters every three minutes, pulverizing minefields, barbed wire and machine gun pits. Mesmerized by the hammering of the enemy, some of the Allied troops walked too close to the falling shells, with the result that the first casualties the 8th Army sustained were men suffering from acute vertigo because they had inhaled the fumes from the strong explosives. The New Zealand infantry reached its objective at 0530, with the tanks crossing to lead the attack at 0615, delayed by half an hour due to problems encountered in clearing the minefields and the low visibility caused by the dust clouds. The Panzer Army had chosen that night to return to Central European Time (from German Summer Time they had been using until then), and this heightened the confusion even more. The RAF continued attacking them and among the targets was the Afrika Korps headquarters, where von Thoma was slightly wounded. Telephone communications were only re-established at 0530 and, even then, Rommel could communicate only with his army's central headquarters.

In the beginning, the Germans thought that the attack was more to the north than where it was actually launched. By 0400, they knew there was a thrust under way on 15th Panzer Division's left but were still under the impression it was a diversion. Only by the morning did the "fog of war" clear for Rommel, although the details still escaped him. He had no contact with von Radow and, consequently, 21st Panzer Division was late in receiving the message ordering it to return adjacent to the Rahman track. Von Thoma met von Vaerst at 15th Panzer Division's headquarters at 0815, where it was arranged for the 21st to strike the enemy from the north, while the 15th, after assembling all the available Italians tanks of the "Littorio" and "Trieste," would launch a simultaneous attack from the west. This combined attack could not start before 1100 so, until then, the Germans would have to content themselves with a defensive line of 24 88 mm anti-tank guns to slow down the Allied advance. As dawn broke, the 9th Armoured Brigade tanks were plainly visible, presenting easy targets for the German gunners, who were patiently waiting at the Rahman track. The British tanks were hit one after another and set on fire, with their crews jumping out of their "brewed up" vehicles and desperately rolling in the sand to extinguish the flames consuming their overalls.

A heavy sandstorm then rose that limited visibility to just 30 meters, increasing confusion and giving a tragic dimension to the already chaotic situation close to the Rahman track. Some of the tanks managed to escape and get close to the German positions, to machine gun and crush a number of unfortunate Germans beneath their tracks. Some of the defenders were put to flight, while others remained in their positions and fought desperately, dying on the desert sand. There were instances of individual heroism when German soldiers, like First Lieutenant Ralf Rinkler of the 104th Mechanized Regiment (Panzergrenadier-Regiment 104), tried to stem the tide of British tanks. He threw a grenade into the open hatch of a Sherman turret, but saw it miss its target and bounce off. The British tank commander sarcastically replied, "Almost!"

The crushing defeat shows in the despondent demeanor of this German soldier who, hiding his face, sits next to a comrade. He is one of the 30,000 Panzer Army Africa troops captured by the Allies.

Casualties on both sides were terrible. The British lost 70 tanks in an hour, but Currie's armored brigade had succeeded in completing its vital mission and creating the breach that Montgomery was waiting for. As planned, 1st Armoured Division's tanks were now rolling down the Rahman track to take over the advance.

Rommel and von Thoma tried tenaciously to block the breach, throwing the 15th and 21st Panzer Divisions into the battle, managing to strike at the Allies with converging blows from two different directions. The fierce exchange of fire lasted throughout the day, with the British Shermans, Grants, and Crusaders fighting almost at point-blank range with the German PzKpfw IIIs and IVs, while they tried to drive them out of Tell el Aqqaqir. The two British brigades engaged in the battle expended enormous quantities of ammunition firing at the German anti-tank guns situated on a lower ridge, succeeding in destroying many of them. By the evening, Panzer Army Africa was left with just 35 German and 100 Italian battle-worthy tanks to face three British armored divisions,

The Daily Mirror's front-page on 5 November 1942. Trumpeting Rommel's defeat at El Alamein.

throwing a flare on his bed. He broke the high jump record. We threw a grenade in one of the trucks and the result was extremely satisfying."

Rommel had to face the blunt truth, despite the bravery of the Afrika Korps, his proud army had been beaten. Italian units were scattering in panic, and the only chance to rescue what remained was to order a withdrawal 100 kilometers to the west and reach the Fuka Line. His mechanized units would form a protective screen, keeping the enemy away at all costs to give the infantry 24 hours to escape. The 90th Light Division's troops, cunningly, roughly buried thousands of metal objects in the sand to delay Montgomery's sappers by confusing the mine detectors.

However, Rommel had not taken into consideration Hitler's will. The next day, the Fuhrer sent him a stern telegram that stated, "In your present situation nothing else can be thought of but to hold on, not to yield a step, and to throw in every weapon and every fighting man…It would not be the first time in history that the stronger will has triumphed over the enemy's stronger battalions. You can show your troops no other road than that of victory or death."

The commande of Panzer Army Africa was forced to order his units to halt the withdrawal, but he did so infuriated by the Wehrmacht High Command's loss of any sense of reality. "This crazy order came in like a shell!" he complained to Field Marshal Kesselring, who arrived on a visit to the front on the morning of 4 November. Holding possession of a small piece of desert had absolutely no military value compared to saving the fighting troops. Hitler, on the other hand, thought only of his prestige when making decisions. He was more

while the precious "88s" were reduced by two-thirds. In addition, Montgomery now revealed another hidden "Ace" in the form of the fresh 4th Indian Division and the 7th Armoured Division and throwing them against the Italian "Trieste" and "Trento" Divisions that quickly disintegrated. A British officer recalled, "Our troops pounced on the enemy's light vehicles like pirates and created havoc in its rear. The Italians looked at us at a loss. They could not believe their eyes, although our artillery barrage continued throughout the night. They approached us with eyes wide open, looked at our berets and then walking away, hesitating, as if they did not believe it to be true and then returning to take another look. …By dawn we passed someone still sleeping in his bed. From the abundance of vehicles and equipment surrounding him, it was clear that he was an Italian supply officer. We woke him up by occupied at that moment with the Battle of Stalingrad that hung in the balance. The last thing he wanted was news of a retreat by the victor of Tobruk back toward Cyrenaica published on the Allied newspapers' front pages. He believed he had invented the cure-all for military failure, based on his experiences of the 1941-1942 winter in Russia, when the Wehrmacht stood firm in front of Moscow after his intervention, and not allowing the Soviets to destroy it in the dangerous withdrawal phase. Rommel must not withdraw one step. What counted was not the difference in men and weapons, but fortitude.

Rommel was not a man to openly disobey a direct order from the Fuhrer; he was an honorable representative of the disciplined German military establishment. Instead, he watched as his forces were destroyed piece by piece throughout 4 November. The Italians were decimated in the south, where XIII Corps struck a crushing blow, while, in the center, the "Ariete" Armored Division, the old Afrika Korps comrade, was crushed by the British Grants and Shermans.

The "Littorio" Armored Division was annihilated, and the "Trieste" Mechanized Division, covering the panzers' southern flank, was put to flight. The Italians had long ceased to be an organized military force, and those with vehicles headed west, leaving their comrades without water or food and ready to surrender. The confusion and breakup of the Italian half of the Panzer Army affected the more disciplined German units. The Scots captured the 15th Panzer Division headquarters, where "they decorated themselves with hundreds of Iron Crosses they discovered in a box." The 9th Australian and the 1st Armoured Divisions reached the coast, after the "Trieste" Division had scattered in all directions, trapping units of the German 164th Infantry Division. Rommel's chief of staff, Colonel Fritz Bayerlein, barely managed to escape and reached the command post at El Daba after walking for two hours in the desert.

The crisis reached its peak, and Rommel decided that he could wait no longer, fighting against an enemy that possessed 20 times more tanks than his own army. Lieutenant General von Thoma commented that "Hitler's order is pure madness" and Rommel, at his own risk, gave the order to retreat to the west. He had already lost

The weapon most feared by the Allied tank crews throughout the war was the "88," the infamous 88 mm anti-aircraft gun that was equally successful when used as an anti-tank weapon.

Because the flat desert terrain afforded no protection against shrapnel, the infantry had to "dig in" at almost every position. This soldier wears the standard tropical uniform with tropical webbing. The dark Waffenfarbe around the shoulder boards could be black, thus indicating that this man is a pioneer. The temporary sand coating on his helmet shows the field gray beneath. (Bundesarchiv)

32,000 men, over 1,000 guns and at least 450 tanks. The next day, Hitler approved the withdrawal, but the same old story of the war in the desert would be repeated. The Axis forces no longer held a short front anchored on firm flanks but a fluid line with its southern flank extremely vulnerable. The 7th Armoured Division had outflanked the Germans before Rommel had time to consolidate his new defensive line and, after a short but fierce exchange of fire, von Thoma's group was destroyed and the general was captured by Captain Allen Grant-Singer of the Reconnaissance Troop, 10th Hussars (Prince of Wales' Own). The retreat turned into a rout, with an immense number of tanks, guns, vehicles, and supplies crudely abandoned along the roads used by the escaping Panzer Army. The long column of a defeated army, winding like a 60-kilometer-long snake on the coastal road, reached el Daba. Even here, there was no time to destroy even its repair shops, a train was abandoned at the railroad station with its engine still running, and the remnants of a once proud army passed Fuka, still ceaselessly harried by the RAF.

Knowledge in hindsight

As Rommel's exhausted troops abandoned the area they had saturated with blood, a weird silence fell on the battlefield, where two well-equipped armies had fought tenaciously for days. For kilometers on end, the desert was strewn with corpses, wreckage, burning tanks, empty shell casings, destroyed guns, Afrika Korps uniforms, pieces of barbed wire, and an endless collection of letters and photographs from the troops' personal belongings. The dead had already turned to black from exposure to the ruthless desert sun and were surrounded by letters from their loved ones back home. "We are so happy you have left the wretched desert and are now in Egypt," a German mother wrote to her son. "May you always be a brave soldier and I hope Saint Dominic will protect you," wrote an Italian wife, with her wishes for her loved one.

Montgomery hoped that he would succeed in capturing the Panzer Army before it could escape. However, his vanguards, now advancing in open country, were confused, and it was extremely difficult for them to find their way in the deep night of a desert where they had not previously reconnoitered. Like their men, the British commanders were also exhausted and felt a sorrow for the price of victory of El Alamein. The 12 days of battle had cost the 8th Army 13,560 dead, wounded, and missing. Major-General D. N. Wimberley of the 51st (Highland) Division, sadly watched as medical personnel collected the bodies of his troops, whispering, "Never again!" while Curry of the 9th Armoured Brigade, sullenly pointed to his 12 remaining tanks when asked where his regiments

A battery of the 44th Artillery Regiment (Motorized) of the 15th Panzer Division fires at advancing enemy tanks from an open field emplacement. The regiment destroyed more than 100 British tanks at Sidi Rezegh on 23 November 1941. The platoon and gun commanders observe the fall of shot. Four gunners struggle to hold down the folding trail spade in the stony ground. (Bundesarchiv)

were, saying , "These are my armored regiments!"

Montgomery, on the other hand, was filled with enthusiasm. Dressed in a gray pullover with khaki trousers (KD slacks) and a silk scarf, he announced to the war correspondents after the end of the battle: "It was a wonderful battle. Complete and absolute victory! The Germans are finished. Finished!" Yet, it was only a half-truth. Rommel succeeded in saving the remnants of his army on the long road of retreat, taking advantage of the torrential rain in the desert of the following days and Montgomery's less-than-spirited pursuit (he did not seem to be in any special hurry after his sweeping victory), and he was yet unaware that he would not stop until reaching Tunisia, 2,100 kilometers distant from fatal El Alamein.

There was a great difference, now, with the 8th Army of the past. Montgomery now had the means to be able to preplan his supplies, which is "nine-tenths of war in the desert" as British officers confessed. This time, 8th Army Engineers repaired destroyed roads, bridges, railroad lines, and the harbors that Rommel had quickly abandoned, while ships were waiting, heavily laden on the open sea, for the signal telling of the capture of Benghazi, to start unloading 3,000 tons of supplies a day. The Allies now had American transport aircraft to move urgent

supplies the great distances from Cairo to El Agheila, and Montgomery was in position to carry on with his advance at a steady pace, neutralizing the deadly booby traps Germans had left behind, stopping only for very few days to fight at El Agheila and Zem Zem.

"The Battle of El Alamein was a resounding victory," British journalists wrote, achieved in time, before Eisenhower's landings at the other end of the Mediterranean. The fact that Rommel's next stop was at the Mareth Line in Tunisia, 2,100 kilometers distant and four months later, is an indication of the totality of the defeat suffered by the "Desert Fox" at El Alamein. Total casualties for the 8th Army was 13,500 men, just under 8 percent of the fighting forces engaged in the battle. Around 500 tanks were out of action, but only 150 were completely destroyed, while 100 guns were lost. The price was definitely not so excessive, if one balances it against what was achieved, yet there are many historians and researchers who argue that Montgomery could have achieved a more "economical" victory if he had taken advantage of his defensive success at Alam Halfa. However, If one takes into consideration the fact that the British armored divisions had been held in check for so long at the Rahman road and Tell el Aqqaqir by a far fewer panzers, it becomes clear that they achieved little better against the Panzer Army in August.

One wonders, could Montgomery have penetrated the enemy front faster and with less cost if he had not attacked in the north, where Axis forces were stronger? Looking at the map, one realizes that if the 8th Army had attacked in the south between Deir el Munassib and Qaret el Himeimat, its forces would have been "channelled" inevitably into the thin neck north of Jebel Kalakh, where Rommel had taken great care to organize a "killing box," covered by his old minefields. The central sector north of Ruweisat Ridge was as well protected and, additionally, it would have given the Afrika Korps the chance to concentrate its dispersed forces faster than it did against the threat in the north. Montgomery broke new ground as far as he could, considering the qualitative difference between the 8th Army troops and staff and that of the Afrika Korps. Rommel and his officers (like Nelson many years before) were so experienced and imbued with a common operational doctrine that their units moved almost by instinct, having a great latitude of initiative even at the lowest echelons. In contrast, the 8th Army had to be guided every step by a firm, decisive leader.

Montgomery's critics accuse him of using overcautious tactics and of being wasteful of lives and matériel because he insisted on launching his attack against the strongest sectors of the enemy defenses instead of following the tactic of indirect approach. There is no doubt that all the Allied divisions engaged in the battle suffered considerable casualties, but they cannot be considered excessive in either infantry or armor. The effect casualties have on morale is not just a matter of numbers. The smaller the combat team (as is the case with armor crews), the larger the effect on morale from comrades' casualties, especially if the

more prominent characters are among the casualties, as is often the case. The comparatively low number of destroyed 8th Army tanks indicates that most of the disabled tanks were the result of mines.

The Germans, too, fought with less than their usual effectiveness and clarity of mind. Rommel's counterattacks, throughout the battle, achieved little except more casualties for his forces. Stumme's tactics may have been more careful, and the local counterattacks he had planned may have cost him less but, even in the best scenario, the only thing they would have achieved would have been the prolonging of the battle for a few days. The outcome of the battle would have been no different. When drawing up his campaign timetable, Montgomery calculated that the battle would last 10 to 12 days, and so planned the initial assault to go in 13 days before Eisenhower's landing, which had been set for 4 November. "Ike," however, postponed his invasion until 8 November. So, whatever the outcome, Rommel would have been forced to fall back on the 17th day, as he would find himself between two enemy armies (the 8th from the east and the 1st from the west), each superior to his own forces. Reliable military analysts agree that even if the Battle of El Alamein had not been fought, Rommel would have been forced to evacuate Egypt in a month's time (from the time of the landings in his rear) and, maybe, Libya in three months. Why, then, did Churchill decide to undertake an unnecessary battle? Was the act of saving British prestige worth the sacrifice of thousands of brave men? War is always a psychologically charged event, apart from a strategic game. The British people and the army were in dire need of a clear victory, a modern

Waterloo against a new Napoleon, before the American GIs actively engaged themselves in the war, and they deservedly earned it.

"All had gone according to the plan," if one is ready to believe Montgomery, but the positioning of the 8th Army units in the battle had serious flaws, mostly after 24 October. Positioning X and XXX Corps with such little distance between them often created traffic congestion and confusion, while the disastrous delay by the New Zealanders on 5 November at the minefield south of Fuka allowed the enemy to escape to fight again. "Monty" was always ready to dismiss any military failure, large or small, from his shining leadership profile that had been so skillfully constructed.

Each well-meaning critic, though, should take into account the fact that the Battle of El Alamein was, perhaps, the one most shrouded in the "fog of war" when compared with many others during World War II, due to the vastness of the landscape it was fought over. The situation must often have seemed chaotic and incredibly confusing for the lowly private soldier, ordered, at times, to attack and then to remain for days in his trench, or for the tank crew slowly crawling through the darkness and dust, avoiding the mines that ever-threatened to blow it to pieces, or trying to avoid the deadly anti-tank guns or enemy armor. The combatants, in many instances, did not know where either friendly or enemy forces were, where the minefields lay, and which was cleared ground. Troops shot at vague targets and were fired on by invisible enemies, while "all attempts to learn what was happening led from some false information to more false information," veterans of the battle often commented. The Allies fought aggressively, however, and succeeded in overpowering a worthy opponent, capable and cunning; the enemy lost because its leaders did not pay enough attention to the struggle.

In just a few days, the legendary 8th Army accomplished an outstanding feat of arms, forcing the Germans, for the first time, to withdraw over a vast distance. It was the turn of the tide, the beginning of the end for the fortunes of Nazi Germany while, at the same time, a victory for British prestige, albeit her swan song as a great, independent world power. "In the grey November morning," Cartier wrote, "bells in London, the ones still standing, mute since 1940, bells that would only toll to announce the German invasion of the island, the bells of London toll for El Alamein."

Afrika Korps infantry in typically featureless desert terrain.

Air forces at El Alamein

During operations in North Africa, many Allied and Axis air force units were in theater in support of ground operations and also to accompany them through advance or retreat. On 23 October 1942, the eve of the Battle of El Alamein, the ratio of available airplanes was about 2:1 in the Allied favor.

Allied air forces

For the British, the Middle East covered an area from the Balkans to East Africa and from Malta to Iraq. General Headquarters, RAF Middle East, was the air force command in theatre with Air Chief Marshal Sir Arthur Tedder in overall command.

In October 1942, the 8th Army had the Western Desert Air Force (WDAF,) later to be better known as the Desert Air Force (DAF), for close air support. It was under the command of Air Vice-Marshal Arthur Coningham, and

its main airfields were in the area of Amriya, close to Alexandria. Montgomery moved his headquarters to the Burg el Arab coast, close to Coningham's, which represented the beginning of a fine period of close cooperation that would fuse the 8th Army and the WDAF into a unified force.

The dedicated teamwork of all involved parties was the basis for implementing air power for ground battle requirements, all under Tedder's overall control. To achieve these aims, Coningham had units from

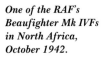

One of the RAF's Beaufighter Mk IVFs in North Africa, October 1942.

An American P-40F of the 87th Fighter Squadron in the North African desert.

Headquarters, RAF Middle East, seconded to him, and on call, although close air support for the 8th Army was WDAF's mission. Wellington, Liberator, Halifax, Marauder, and Boston bombers flew hundreds of sorties over the enemy's rear areas. Wellingtons and Beauforts were sinking Afrika Korps supply ships with remarkable accuracy and were regularly bombing its supply ports, giving, as time went by, a significant advantage to the 8th Army. The Fleet Air Arm (FAA) squadrons, equipped with Albacores, Swordfish, Fulmars, Hurricanes, and Walruses, engaged in naval cooperation, convoy, and reconnaissance missions, etc. Additionally, Coningham could use Headquarters, RAF Middle East, transport, rescue, strategic reconnaissance, and meteorological

reconnaissance squadrons. At his disposal in October 1942 were the WDAF's 609 operational aircraft in addition to the aircraft Headquarters, RAF Middle East, placed at his disposal, making a total of more than 1,000 aircraft. The first United States Army Air Forces (USAAF) squadrons arrived in the Middle East, under Major General Lewis H. Brereton, before the Battle of El Alamein. Three P-40 Warhawk squadrons arrived in the region at the end of July, and four

Supermarine Spitfire Mk. V, ER228/ZX-S, No. 145 Squadron, RAF, Western Desert Air Force, 1942. Dark Earth and Mid Stone upper surfaces, Azure Blue undersides. Black spinner, codes edged in white.

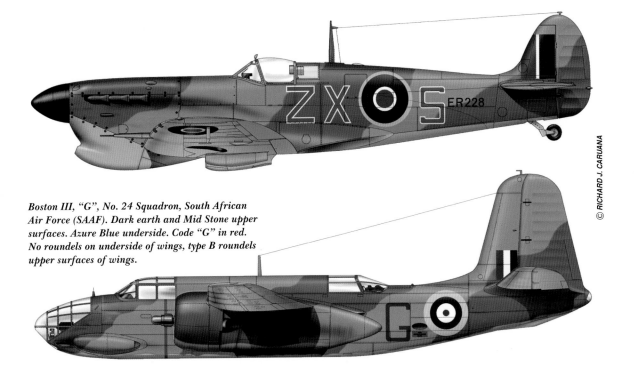

Boston III, "G", No. 24 Squadron, South African Air Force (SAAF). Dark earth and Mid Stone upper surfaces. Azure Blue underside. Code "G" in red. No roundels on underside of wings, type B roundels upper surfaces of wings.

© RICHARD J. CARUANA

A 20 mm Flakvierling 38 crew rapidly brings its gun into action as enemy aircraft approach. A very effective weapon against low-flying aircraft, this one is probably operated by one of the light companies of the 33rd Flak Regiment.

No. 112 Squadron, RAF, famous for its "Sharkmouth" Kittyhawk Mk. IIIs. By October 1942, Kittyhawks (the British name for the American P-40 Warhawk) had replaced the obsolete Tomahawk Mk. IIB (P-40C). It was fitted with a more powerful engine in a redesigned nose and armed with six .303-caliber machine guns. The WDAF had 10 Kittyhawk/Warhawk squadrons in October 1942, used mainly for close support missions.

B-24 Liberator squadrons and four B-25 Mitchell squadrons during the next month. A review of the control of these forces was needed, following this increase of American presence in the Middle East. So, operational control of heavy bombers was placed in American hands, while medium-bomber and fighter squadrons were under the control of the RAF. For closer cooperation, an American headquarters was set up close to Coningham's advanced headquarters.

The Allied air forces comprised many of many different nationalities, including British, Canadians, South Africans, Australians, Americans, Dutch, French, and Greeks, using a variety of different equipment. While each was accountable to its own government, it was still a cohesive, reliable force, thanks to Tedder's coordination of these air forces and to their inspired tactical use by Coningham. Training for the coming battle was systematized, stressing signals communication and discipline, in order to achieve this common goal. Special training was required for the crews of two American Boston squadrons as they were tasked with the difficult job of laying smokescreens from the air. Two South African Air Force Hurricane Mk. IID squadrons

Hurricanes were the workhorse of the WDAF fighter force during the Battle of El Alamein, equipping 13 squadrons. The Hurricane Mk. IIC (Trop) was normally fitted with four 20 mm cannons, but three of the aircraft in this photo (No. 94 Squadron, RAF) appear to have been equipped with only two of the four in order to save weight. Under the nose there is a tropical air filter. The Hurricane's performance was inferior to the Bf 109F/G, but its robust construction and wide undercarriage allowed it to operate from emergency landing grounds.

were equipped as "tank-busters," fitted with 40 mm cannons and carrying armor-piercing shells. They had to hit their target directly and as quickly as possible if their attack was to be successful, as their low flight made them susceptible as targets for all large- or small-caliber enemy weapons. After a period of long, intensive training, resulting in many casualties, they began operating along the front's southern sector.

Coningham organized WDAF operations so it could fly missions that would follow the battle conditions as they developed. His goal, before the attack, was to lessen the chances of the

enemy bombing troop concentration areas. Day and night missions against enemy airfields, air cover over the ground forces' advance positions, and ongoing reconnaissance of the enemy's defense positions helped frustrate the enemy from bombing the Allies.

The first attacks, by Baltimores and Bostons, were made on 19 October, and their targets were airfields in the area of El Daba. Night raids by Bostons followed, with the targets being illuminated by flare-dropping FAA Albacores. The Italian airfields at Fuka and El Daba were the next day's targets. Fuka was an easy target, as it was just a five-minute flight from El

The first B-24D Liberators in the Middle East were originally destined for China, but ended up in the 1st (Provisional) Bombardment Group of the United States Army, Middle East Air Force. In June 1942, they were reinforced by the 98th (Heavy) Bombardment Group, one of which is seen here flying over the desert. They operated out of Palestine beginning in August, then from Egypt and finally from Libya. Two RAF squadrons were equipped with the same type. Liberators were used as strategic bombers against Rommel's supply lines and, in October 1942, there were 107 operational aircraft.

COMPARATIVE TABLE OF FIGHTERS

	TYPE	ENGINE	MAXIMUM SPEED (km/h)	ARMAMENT / BOMB LOAD	OPERATIONAL CEILING (m)	RATE OF CLIMB (m/min)	MAXIMUM RANGE (km)
ALLIES	Hawker Hurricane IIB	RR Merlin XX, 1,280 hp	550	12 x 7.7 mm 2 x 227 kg	11,125	825	772
	Curtiss Kittyhawk Mk. IA P-40E Warhawk	Allison V-1710-39, 1,150 hp	582	6 x 12.7 mm 1 x 113 kg	8,900	872	1,370
	Supermarine Spitfire VB	RR Merlin 45, 1,440 hp	602	2 x 20 mm 4 x 7.7 mm 1 x 227 kg	11,277	1,145	758
AXIS	Messerschmitt Bf 109F-4	DB 601E, 1,300 hp	628	1 x 20 mm 2 x 7.92 mm	12,000	1,346	707
	Messerschmitt Bf 109G-6	DB 605A, 1,475 hp	621	1 x 30 mm 2 x 13 mm 1 x 250 kg	11,750	1,430	726
	Messerschmitt Bf 110C-4	2 x DB 610N, 1,200 hp	560	2 x 20 mm 5 x 7.92 mm 4 x 250 kg	10,000	679	774
	Fiat CR.42 Falco	Fiat A74R, 840 hp	430	2 x 12.7 mm 2 x 100 kg	10,500	753	775
	Fiat G.50 bis Freccia	Fiat A74R, 870 hp	470	2 x 12.7 mm 2 x 100 kg	8,840	815	1,000
	Macchi MC.200 Saetta	Fiat A74, 870 hp	501	2 x 12.7 mm 2 x 160 kg	8,900	980	570
	Macchi C. 202 Folgore	DB 601A-1, 1,175 hp	594	2 x 12.7 mm 1 x 7.7 mm 2 x 160 kg	11,500	1,176	765

COMPARATIVE TABLE OF BOMBERS

	TYPE	ENGINE	MAXIMUM SPEED (km/h)	BOMB LOAD (kg)	CREW	OPERATIONAL CEILING (m)	MAXIMUM RANGE (km)
ALLIES	Martin Baltimore IV	2 x Wright Cyclone R-2600-19, 1,660 hp	486	907	4	7,315	1,700
	Douglas Boston III	2 x Wright GR-2600-A, 1,500 hp	560	907	3	7,720	1,610
	North American B-25C Mitchell	2 x Wright R-2600-13, 1,700 hp	459	1,361	6	7,315	2,414
	Vickers Wellington Mk. IC	2 x Bristol Pegasus XVIII, 1,050 hp	410	2,041	5	6,710	3,450
	Consolidated B-24 Liberator	4 x P & W R-1830-65, 1,200 hp	467	3,629	8 – 9	8,534	3,540
AXIS	Junkers Ju 87D-1/Trop	1 x Junkers Jumo 211, 1,400 hp	408	1,800	2	7,390	1,000
	Caproni Ca.311	2 x Piaggio P.XVI RC35, 650 hp	365	400	3	7,400	1,600
	Savoia Marchetti SM.79 Sparviero	3 x Alfa Romeo 126 RC34, 780 hp	590	1,250	4 – 5	7,000	1,890
	Cant Z.1007 Alcione	3 x Piaggio P.XI bis RC40, 1,000 hp	448	3,000	5	8,100	1,280

Alamein. Baltimores and Kittyhawks were used for the first time as dive-bombers on a wide front, leaving 13 destroyed aircraft in their wake. The Wellingtons went into action on 21 October. Bombing missions continued unceasingly, day and night, until the eve of the battle. The WDAF flew a variety of missions during the night before the attack: illuminating enemy defensive positions by flare-dropping, bombing fortified artillery positions, low level attacks on enemy concentration areas, jamming enemy communications with specially equipped Wellingtons, and creating confusion with smoke screens and dummy paratroop drops. Before the beginning of the attack, while the artillery barrage was in full swing, 48 Wellingtons dropped 125 tons of bombs on enemy positions and, when the attack began, emphasis was placed on attacking enemy troops in those areas where the battle was most

intense, with the maximum number of aircraft available. During 23 October, fighters filled the sky, patrolling over the Axis airfields, and maintaining complete air superiority.

The Baltimores, Bostons, and fighter-bombers were a familiar sight to the troops on the ground across all sectors of the front that needed air support, throughout the operations. On the 26th October, WDAF reconnaissance aircraft, with fighter escort, noticed enemy troop concentrations as he prepared to counterattack and led waves of Baltimores and Mitchells in cooperation with the artillery bombardment in breaking them up. On 31 October, numerous WDAF fighter-bomber sorties struck at enemy tanks that were attacking Allied positions, causing significant numbers of enemy casualties. The next day, 68 Wellingtons and 19 Albacores began a seven-hour bombardment of

Kittyhawk Mk. I, No. 112 Squadron, RAF, Desert Air Force. Dark Earth and Mid Stone upper surfaces, Azure Blue undersides. Black spinner and white codes. Note "London Pride" motto above "Y code.

Curtiss P-40F, 41-13696/5-5, 65th Fighter Squadron, 57th Fighter Group, Egypt. Sand (FS.30279) upper surfaces and Neutral Gray (FS.36173) undersides. Red spinner and code "55" on the nose. Code "5-5" on the fuselage white with black shadow. Yellow serial number on vertical stabilizer. National markings on the upper surface of the left wing and the underside of the right wing.

© RICHARD J. CARUANA

enemy positions in the areas of Tell el Aqqaqir, Sidi Abd el Rahman and on the enemy's rear, destroying many supply dumps and his communication network. The bombing intensified until the Axis began its withdrawal. On 2 November, bombers dropped 165 tons of bombs, mostly on enemy positions on the Rahman road, where the front was to be breached. On 3 November, Allied air force operations reached their peak, with the main area of operations concentrating in the north from early morning. WDAF pilots achieved 1,208 sorties in the 24 hours that followed, contributing to the Axis decision to fall back. Provisions were made to fill the need for nonstop support for the 8th Army after it had breached the enemy's frontline. The WDAF organized a mobile, instantly available force, comprising the 17 British and American fighter squadrons of 211 Group. This force (Force A) was WDAF's spearhead, pursuing the enemy, taking off from forward airfields formerly occupied by the enemy and captured by the infantry. The eight Hurricane squadrons of 212 Group (including the Greek No. 335 Squadron) formed Force B that protected the air space, mostly behind the front.

Throughout this time, WDAF's unsung heroes were not only the ground crews. A range of impressive administrative and repair services, squadrons with special workshops and aircraft recovery vehicles etc., developed behind the combat squadrons. The air raids continued ceaselessly, thanks to the sufficient number of aircraft made available by the maintenance units. No. 103 Maintenance Unit (at Aboukir, Egypt) was the most famous of these support units. This unit built an effective air filter (known as the Aboukir filter) that was used by the majority of the Spitfires operating in the Middle East.

Axis air forces

Following Italy's entry into the war in June 1940, the needs of the Royal Italian Air Force (Regia Aeronautica, RA) in North Africa increased dramatically, and new units reinforced the ones already in the theater. A new high command was formed, 5th Air Fleet (5a Squadra Aerea), and all Italian air forces in the theater were placed under its command. Correspondingly, when German air units were sent to the area in February 1941, Air Commander Africa (Fliegerführer Afrika) took over

A brace of Messerschmitt Bf 110s of 9/ZG 26 fly over the North African coast. They carry underwing drop tanks, a normal procedure for over-water flights.

A pair of SM.79 Sparviero bombers of the Royal Italian Air Force.

tactical command of the Luftwaffe air forces.

The defensive role played by the Axis air forces was forced on them by the Allies, and by the inability of the Deutsche Afrika Korps (DAK) to undertake offensive operations after September 1942. In addition, the qualitative superiority of German aircraft compared to Italian ones led them to be concentrated mostly in the front line area while RA units were to the west, from the front line to Tripoli. At El Alamein, the Axis forces mainly had to rely on a fighter and bomber force that was faced with hundreds of air raids behind their lines. If vigilance slackened, aircraft could be destroyed on the ground when the Allies attacked an airfield. To counteract this, each day the fighter squadrons alternately undertook to have two or three aircraft at readiness, which meant that they had to able to take off in 30 seconds. The Germans deployed a central intercept system, and each squadron also had its own local "early warning system." The intercept controller plotted each enemy air raid and the course of the intercepting forces and directed aircraft in the air. Although the Luftwaffe fully cooperated with the RA, the Italians also maintained their own operations room and control system, to which a German liaison officer was attached.

Until the summer of 1942, the opposing air forces followed the swing

A Ju 88 on a Libyan airfield.

A Macchi MC.202 Folgore preserved in the National Air and Space Museum, Washington, D.C. Painted in the scheme flown by Master Sergeant (Sergente Maggiore) Amleto Monterumici of 90a Squadriglia, 10o Gruppo, 4o Stormo. The wing operated from North African airfields from April 1942 to January 1943. 5a Squadra Aerea had 93 MC.202s on the eve of the Battle of El Alamein.

of the pendulum the ground forces drew between Tripolitania and Egypt. When the front was stabilized at El Alamein in October, air commander Africa, Major General H. Seidelmann, had at his disposal less than 129 aircraft. The Luftwaffe fighter force consisted mainly of Bf 109F-4 Trop and the newer Bf 109G-6 Trop aircraft. These aircraft were improved versions of the Bf 109E, fitted with more powerful engines and increased firepower, including a 20mm or 30 mm cannon firing through the airscrew hub. Each "trop" aircraft was fitted with an additional air filter that reduced its maximum speed by less than 5 percent. In contrast, the air filters fitted to the Hurricanes at that time reduced their speed by 8 percent. Nevertheless, Allied air supremacy

became, little by little, more apparent, even though the Luftwaffe was using improved aircraft types. Pilots had to fly multiple daily missions, and the new pilots had no time for battle training or to improve their techniques or even to acclimatize themselves to the new climatic conditions, before being thrown into the battle.

Spitfires began arriving in numbers in North Africa, and their air raids, strafing, or bombing of airfields caused a steady rise in the number of destroyed or damaged German aircraft, either on the ground or in the air. Most of the available Bf 109s equipped the 27th Fighter Wing (JG 27 "Afrika") – equivalent to a RAF Group - that had been in Africa since the beginning of operations. Even during the Battle of Al Alamein, many squadrons rotated between North Africa and Italy or Russia, but, excluding casualties, the Bf 109 force was maintained at 12 to 15 squadrons. Their missions were mainly of a defensive nature, confronting the numerous Allied fighter-bombers or medium bombers and their fighter escorts or acting as fighter cover for the Stuka dive bombers and the Italian Air Force's offensive missions. While they achieved a high kill-loss ratio in aerial combat, the final result was never in doubt. On 27 October, 63 aircraft took part in the Axis' largest counterattack. Although the fighter escort minimized their casualties to just five aircraft, only four managed to reach their target area. Not all fighters operating in North Africa during this period were single engine. Two squadrons of Ju 88C-6 and Ju 88A-4 Trop were detached at Barce, while a Bf 110 squadron was based at Derna.

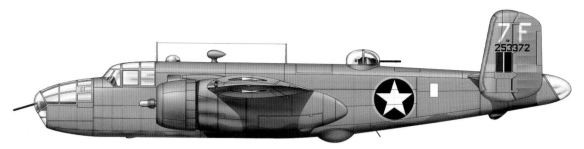

B-25C-NA Mitchell, 42-53372/7F, 487th Bomber Squadron, 340th Bomber Group, 9th Air Force. Sand (FS.30279) upper surfaces and Neutral Gray (FS.36173) undersides. Standard six position national markings, edged in yellow. RAF flash added on the vertical tail unit.

Hawker Hurricane Mk.IIC, HL887/AK-W, No. 213 Squadron, RAF. Dark Earth and Mid Stone upper surfaces, Azure Blue undersides. Codes in white. This aircraft carries just one 20 mm cannon in each wing.

Bristol Beaufighter, T4767/BT-T, No. 252 Squadron, RAF, Desert Air Force. Dark Earth and Mid Stone upper surfaces and Azure Blue undersides. Codes in Medium Gray.

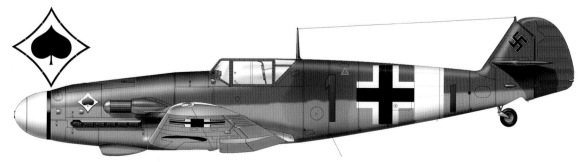

Messerschmitt Bf 109G-2/Trop "Red 1," III/JG 53, October 1942. Sand Brown (Sandbraun, RLM 79) upper surfaces, the rest of the surfaces Light Blue (Hellblau, RLM 65). White spinner, edged in black, white fuselage band and wingtips. Red (RLM 23) number "1" and vertical stripe edged in black on the rear of the fuselage. The overspray behind the cockpit is barely visible.

A Messerschmitt Bf 109F-4/Trop of II/JG 27. Its wing insignia is visible on the nose, and its air filter is closed. The new Bf 109 versions were superior to the Allied types, although this advantage was lost at low levels, where they were usually engaged by the Allied fighters. The photo shows the F4's MG FF 20 mm auto cannon firing through the propeller boss.

The Nazi flag was used as a marker for aircraft. (Bundesarchiv)

outperformed the Bf 110, but the German aircraft had superior firepower, four machine guns, and two cannons, grouped in its nose and could easily destroy an enemy target. The whole of St.G. 3 operated in North Africa, supporting the Afrika Korps, with its Stukas acting as aerial artillery. In October, the strength of the wing amounted to 95 Ju 87D Trop aircraft. Sometimes, the Ju 87s were staged at Siwa Oasis, on the southernmost end of the front and operated from landing grounds there. The Stuka missions included close support for the ground troops in the desert as well as attacking the seaborne supply convoys to Malta. They flew almost daily from their landing fields at Haggag el Quasaba (150 kilometers from El Alamein). They continued aggressively attacking troop concentrations, artillery positions, and armor bivouacs; they even bombed minefields in order to open safe lanes through them, despite being vulnerable, even by the standards of North Africa. The rapid rise in their casualty rates is not surprising when the steady increase in Allied fighter strength is taken into consideration.

The Luftwaffe began using fighters to carry bombs (Jabos) to compensate

Their duties included ground forces close support, escorting convoys and transport aircraft carrying supplies, intercepting allied bomber formations, and reconnaissance. The October casualties were not replaced, as by then the Russian front had priority over the Ju 88s. The Hurricane

A Fiat G.50bis of 352 Squadriglia (Squadron) flies over the desert. Its open cockpit was a common feature of Italian aircraft of the time. The engine of this one is equipped with a filter, although it took the Italians a long time before they fitted filters against the ingestion of sand during takeoff and landing, resulting in a very short engine life. The RA squadrons were equipped with around 90 G.50s before the Battle of El Alamein.

The Cant Z.506 Airone was a successful floatplane, a derivative of the Z.1007 bomber. Its attributes were a long duration and the ability to carry 1,200 kilograms of bombs or torpedoes. It was used primarily for reconnaissance, operating along the coast and over the sea.

for the shortcomings of the Stukas. The Africa Fighter Bomber Group (Jabogruppe Afrika) pilots flew their Bf 109F-4 Trops carrying bombs in close-support operations for the ground forces. These fighter-bombers could approach their targets with a fighter escort and then, after releasing their bombs, could defend themselves on their return to base. Attacking at low level was especially hazardous in North Africa as the troops in the desert defended themselves and returned fire with whatever weapon was at hand, in contrast to the passive attitude of troops on other fronts when attacked by aircraft. The unit's

casualties rose rapidly, but because its missions were extremely important, it was constantly supplied with new aircraft. This group remained active until November. The RA added almost 400 aircraft from the 5th Air Fleet under Lieutenant General (Generale di Squadra Aerea) Felice Porro.

RA had a large number of fighters of different types and capacities, but they were all underpowered and had inferior firepower. The Macchi MC. 200s (a contemporary design to that of the Hurricane and Spitfire) and the Fiat G.50s with the Italian-made Fiat 840 hp engines had begun to show signs of extensive wear and had

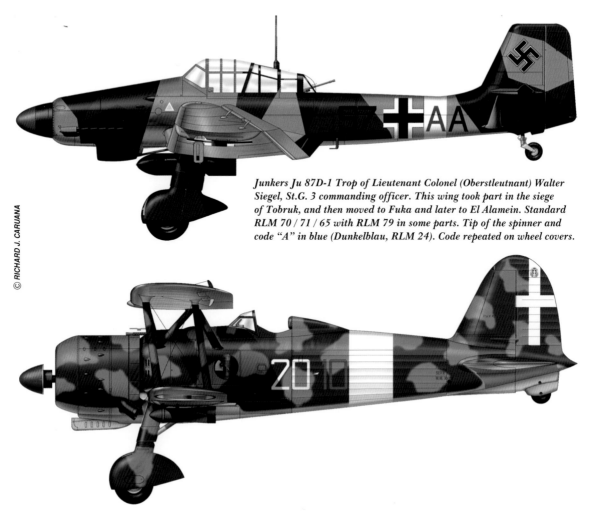

© RICHARD J. CARUANA

Junkers Ju 87D-1 Trop of Lieutenant Colonel (Oberstleutnant) Walter Siegel, St.G. 3 commanding officer. This wing took part in the siege of Tobruk, and then moved to Fuka and later to El Alamein. Standard RLM 70 / 71 / 65 with RLM 79 in some parts. Tip of the spinner and code "A" in blue (Dunkelblau, RLM 24). Code repeated on wheel covers.

Fiat CR.42 "20-10," 20a Squadriglia, 156o Gruppo, 25o Stormo d' Assalto. Dark Olive Green (Verde Oliva Scuro 2) with large swathes of Light Chestnut (Nocciola Chiaro 4) on the upper surfaces. Light Blue/Gray (Grigio Azzuro Chiaro 1) undersurfaces. White fuselage band and code "20," red spinner and code "10." Bombs visible under the wings.

been withdrawn from front-line service. Most of these aircraft had bomb racks fitted and took over ground forces support missions, equipping support wings and independent squadrons.

The Italians also had a large number of CR.42AS biplanes (AS – Africa Settentrionale – signifying the type's modification for service in North Africa) operating in the theater. Already an obsolete design and with outdated airframes in October 1942, they were fitted with bomb racks and their service life was extended. The type was used by six squadrons in Cyrenaica for close support, as a night fighter or for bombing (without success), reconnaissance duties, convoy

escort, etc., while two further groups ventured to operate from Egypt close to the front-line. From July 1942, two more squadrons were equipped with CR.42s and missioned with the task of protecting the oases in southern Libya as the Sahara Aviation Battalion (Battaglione Aviazione Sahariana). In contrast to the types mentioned above, when the first C.202s (powered by the DB601A-1 engines like the Bf 109s) appeared in the skies over North Africa, the Allied pilots were given an unpleasant surprise and those who fought against them were impressed by their performance. The Hurricanes were, suddenly, in an inferior position, and even the newly arrived Spitfire Mk Vs had trouble managing.

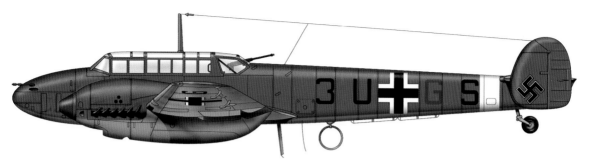

Messerschmitt Bf 110C, 8./ZG 26 in North Africa, around the end of 1942. Painted in blue (Hellblau, RLM 78) and Sand Brown (Sandbrawn RLM 79). White rear fuselage band, red spinners and code "G." Code repeated on the underside of the wing.

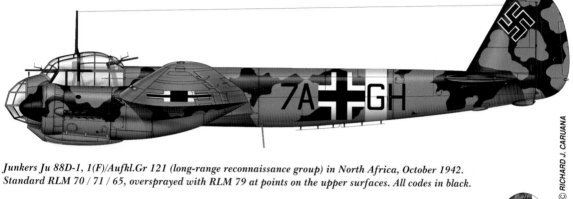

Junkers Ju 88D-1, 1(F)/Aufkl.Gr 121 (long-range reconnaissance group) in North Africa, October 1942. Standard RLM 70 / 71 / 65, oversprayed with RLM 79 at points on the upper surfaces. All codes in black.

© RICHARD J. CARUANA

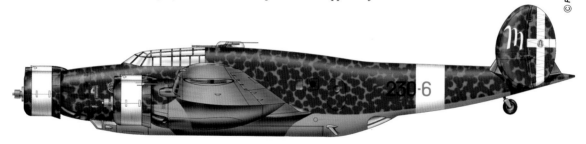

Cant Z.1007bis, 230a Squadriglia, 95o Gruppo, 35o Stormo. The Light Chestnut (Nocciola Chiaro 4) mottle effect was applied over a Dark Olive Green (Verde Oliva Scuro 2) base on the upper surfaces. Light Blue/Gray (Grigio Azzuro Chiaro 4) undersides. The white engine cowlings were used by the aircraft for its service in the Balkans but were still applied on arrival in Africa in June 1942, where the unit served until the fall of the El Alamein defense line.

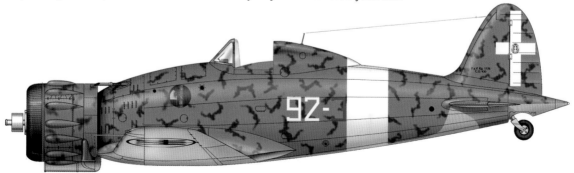

Macchi C.200, 92a Squadriglia, 8o Gruppo, 2o Stormo. Light Chestnut (Nocciola Chiaro 4) upper surfaces with Dark Olive Green (Verde Oliva Scuro 2) irregular rings. Light Blue/Gray (Grigio Azzuro Chiaro 4) undersurfaces. White rear fuselage band and code "92," red code "3." The unit took part in the Axis offensive against El Alamein, after having arrived at Abu Hagag in Egypt.

However, as with all Italian aircraft, the type was also plagued by inferior firepower. In addition, the aerial tactics used by Italian pilots were those of World War I, with aircraft taking up position around the leader and then operating like a big group, without any order or organization. Modern tactics were adopted by very few Italian pilots, and then only by those who had the opportunity to train with the Luftwaffe. Moreover, the few C.202s were forced to undertake missions other types could not. The ones able to carry bombs were used for ground forces support, while the ones equipped with cameras and drop tanks were used as reconnaissance aircraft. The many types of aircraft in the RA's inventory created huge maintenance problems, and there were never enough spares. An indication of this is that the average ratio of availability for Italian aircraft in September was 60 percent, while he RAF's fluctuated from 73 percent to 77 percent. The RA also had a small strategic force, comprising 25 Cant. Z.1007bis bombers and 34 SM.79 torpedo planes with a further 24 Caproni Ca.311 light bombers completing the force.

The Cant Z.1007 proved to be one of the most capable Italian bombers, although just one squadron was equipped with them in North Africa. Their one disadvantage was that they were of wooden construction, which did not stand up well to the rigors and environment of the North African Theater. The SM.79, in contrast, was used successfully and attained a high reputation, mostly due to the enormous courage of their crews. However, all these bombers had common disadvantages: There was no designated navigator, which meant that other crew members had to fulfill this task; their small bomb load was often ineffective, and communication between aircraft was by Morse code and not by radio.

A common practice among the Axis forces was to give control of tactical reconnaissance aircraft to ground force commanders. The Luftwaffe had two reconnaissance squadrons in North Africa: one equipped with the modified Bf 109F-4/R-3s and Bf 110C-4/Rs for tactical reconnaissance, and the other with the Ju 88D Trop for strategic reconnaissance. The RA used the Cant Z.501 flying boats and Cant Z.506

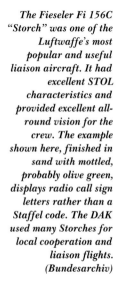

The Fieseler Fi 156C "Storch" was one of the Luftwaffe's most popular and useful liaison aircraft. It had excellent STOL characteristics and provided excellent all-round vision for the crew. The example shown here, finished in sand with mottled, probably olive green, displays radio call sign letters rather than a Staffel code. The DAK used many Storches for local cooperation and liaison flights. (Bundesarchiv)

floatplanes for naval reconnaissance and rescue missions, with great success, as well as Caproni Ca.309s over the desert, while the few SM.79 and Z.1007bis bombers undertook strategic reconnaissance.

Conclusion

Air supremacy was, undoubtedly, one of the many reasons behind the British victory at El Alamein. From the beginning of the battle, the Allied air forces could replace their casualties and reinforce the squadrons already in the front line. Although the skill and capabilities of the opposing pilots were, more or less equal, the Axis pilots flew under debilitating mental and physical conditions and in each encounter were outnumbered (the Italians also qualitatively). The morale factor was more important than the statistical and material results of the opposing forces. The sight of the perfect formations of the Allied aircraft, covering the sky with a majestic indifference, had a strong influence on the Axis front-line soldier, while creating the opposite feelings on their counterparts on the other side.

AIR COMMANDER AFRICA (FLIEGERFÜHRER AFRIKA), GERMANY			
WINGS	**GROUPS**	**SQUADRONS**	**AIRCRAFT TYPE**
JG 27	I./JG 27 (from 25 October)	1./JG 27, 2./JG 27, 3./JG 27	Bf 109F-4/Trop, Bf 109G
	II./JG 27	4./JG 27, 5./JG 27, 6./JG 27	
	III./JG 27	7./JG 27, 8./JG 27, 9./JG 27	
	III./JG 53	7./JG 53, 8./JG 53, 9./JG 53	Bf 109F-4/Trop
St.G. 3	I./ St.G. 3	1./St.G. 3, 2./St.G. 3, 3./St.G. 3	Ju 87D-3/Trop, D-1/Trop
	II./St.G. 3	4./St.G. 3, 5./St.G. 3, 6./St.G. 3	
	III./St.G. 3	7./St.G. 3, 8./St.G. 3, 9./St.G. 3	
	Jabogruppe	10.(Jabo)/JG 27	Bf 109F-4/Trop
	Afrika	10.(Jabo)/JG 53	
Koluft Panzer-Armee Afrika		12./LG 1	Ju 88A-4/Trop
		8./ZG 26	Bf 110
		10./ZG 26	Do 17Z, Ju 88C-6
		4.(H)/Aufkl.Gr. 12	Bf 109F-4/R3,
		1.(F)/Aufkl.Gr. 121	Bf 110C-4/R
			Ju 88D/C Trop

The two reconnaissance squadrons under Panzer Army Africa Air Command (Koluft Panzer-Armee Afrika) were for ground forces cooperation. Additionally, the following units were available for Air Commander Africa: a headquarters squadron (Stabs-Staffel), a courier squadron (Kurierstaffel), and the readiness squadron (Flugbereitschaft) with various aircraft types (Bf 108, Bf 110, C.445, Do 17, Fh 104, Fi 156, Ju 88.)

JG (Jagdgeschwader): fighter wing
St.G. (Sturzkampfgeschwader): dive bomber wing
LG (Lehrgeschwader): operational training wing
ZG (Zerstörergeschwader): heavy fighter (twin-engined) aircraft wing
(H)/Aufkl.Gr.: short-range reconnaissance group
(F)/Aufkl.Gr. (Fernaufklarungsgruppe): long-range reconnaissance group

GERMAN AIRCRAFT TOTAL: 125 Bf 109, 95 Ju 87, 19 Bf 110, 14 Ju 88.

WESTERN DESERT AIR FORCE, GREAT BRITAIN			
GROUPS	**WINGS**	**UNIT**	**AIRCRAFT TYPE**
	No. 3 (SAAF) Wing	Nos. 12 (SAAF), 24 (SAAF) Sqns	Boston III
		No. 21 (SAAF) Sqn	Baltimore I/II/III
	No. 232 Wing, RAF	No. 55, 223 Sqns, RAF	Baltimore I/II/III
		82nd, 83rd, 443rd B.S (USAAF) attached	B-25 Mitchell
	No. 285 Wing, RAF	No. 2 P.R.U., RAF	Spitfire VB
		No. 40 (SAAF) Sqn	Hurricane I/IIA/B
		No. 60 (SAAF) Sqn	Maryland
		No. 208 Sqn, RAF	Hurricane IIA/B
		No. 1437 Flight, RAF	Baltimore I/II/III
No. 211 Group, RAF		Nos. 6 (SAAF), 7 (SAAF) Sqns	Hurricane IID
		64th, 65th F.S. (USAAF) attached	P-40 Warhawk
	No. 233 Wing, RAF	Nos. 2 (SAAF), 4 (SAAF) Sqns	Kittyhawk I/II/III
		No. 5 (SAAF) Sqn	Tomahawk
		No. 260 Sqn, RAF	Kittyhawk I/II
	No. 239 Wing, RAF	Nos. 3 (SAAF), 112, RAF, 250, RAF, 450 (RAAF) Sqns	Kittyhawk I/II/III
		66th F.S. (USAAF) attached	P-40 Warhawk
	No. 244 Wing, RAF	No. 73 Sqn, RAF	Hurricane IIC
		No. 92 Sqn, RAF	Spitfire VB/C
		Nos. 145, RAF, 601, RAF Sqns	Spitfire VB
No. 212 Group, RAF	No. 7 (SAAF) Wing	No. 80 Sqn, RAF	Hurricane IIC
		Nos. 127, RAF, 335 (Hellenic) Sqns	Hurricane IIB
		No. 274 Sqn, RAF	Huricane IIE
	No. 243 Wing, RAF	Nos. 1 (SAAF), 35, RAF, 213, RAF, 238, RAF Sqns	Hurricane IIC
	12th Medium Bombardment Group (USAAF)	81st B.S., 82nd B.S., 83rd B.S., 434th B.S. (Medium) (Medium)	B-25 Mitchell

Only six WDAF wings were organized in Groups. Additionally, the following units were available to reinforce WDAF in support of "Lightfoot," although not under its control:
No. 1 Air Ambulance Unit, RAF, (DH 86 aircraft), No. 162 Sqn, RAF, (Wellington IC)
From No. 201 Group, RAF: Nos. 252, 272 Sqns, RAF, (Beaufighter IC/VIF), Nos. 821 (FAA), 826 (FAA) Sqns (Albacore)
From No. 203 Group RAF: No. 15 (SAAF) Sqn (Blenheim V/Bisley)
From No. 205 Group, RAF: No. 231 Wing, RAF, (Nos 37, 70 Sqns., RAF, with Wellington IC), No. 236 Wing, RAF (Nos. 108, 148 Sqns, RAF, with Wellington IC), No. 238 Wing, RAF (No. 40 Sqn, RAF with Wellington IC and No 104 Sqn, RAF, with Wellington II)
From No. 216 Group, RAF: Nos. 117 (Hudson VI,) 173 (Boston III / Lodestar,) 216 (Bombay / Hudson III / Hudson IV / Lodestar,) and 267 (Hudson III / VI / Lodestar / Dakota) Sqns., RAF.

F.S.: Fighter Squadron
B.S.: Bomber Squadron
PRU: Photographic reconnaissance unit
RAAF: Royal Australian Air Force
RAF: Royal Air Force
SAAF: South African Air Force
USAAF: United States Army Air Forces

ALLIED AIRCRAFT TOTAL: 250 Hurricane, 55 P-40 Warhawk, 55 Spitfire, 45 Kittyhawk, 160 Wellington, 90 B-24 Liberator, 50 B-25 Mitchell, 75 A-30 Baltimore, 35 A-20 Boston, 50 Beaufighter, 40 Blenheim, 30 Beaufort

\multicolumn{4}{c}{**5th AIR FLEET (5A SQUADRA AEREA), ITALY**}			
STORMO (WING)	**GRUPPO** (GROUP)	**SQUADRIGLIE** (SQUADRONS)	**AIRCRAFT TYPE**
2o Stormo	8o Gruppo CT	92a, 93a, 94a	MC.200
	13o Gruppo CT	77a, 78a, 82a	MC.200
3o Stormo	18o Gruppo CT	83a, 85a, 95a	MC.200
	23o Gruppo CT	709a, 74a, 75a	MC.202
4o Stormo	9o Gruppo CT	73a, 96a, 97a	MC.202
	10o Gruppo CT	84a, 90a, 91a	MC.202
15o Stormo	46o Gruppo d' Assalto	20a, 21a	CR.42AS
	47o Gruppo d' Assalto	53a, 54a	CR.42 AS
18o Stormo	37o Gruppo BT	47a, 48a	SM.82
	66o Gruppo OA	87a, 131a	Ca.311
21o Stormo	68o Gruppo OA	24a, 33a	Ca.311, Ca.312
35o Stormo	86o Gruppo BT	190a, 191a	Cant Z.1007
	95o Gruppo BT	380a, 390a, 391a	Cant Z.1007
53o Stormo	150o Gruppo CT	363a, 364a, 365a	MC.200, MC.202
	1o Gruppo Aviazione Presidio Coloniale	12a, 103a, 104a	Ca.309
	101a Gruppo BaT	208a, 238a	CR.42
	131o Gruppo Aerosilurante	279a, 284a	SM.79sil
	133o Gruppo Aerosilurante	174a, 175a	SM.79sil
	145o Gruppo T	604a, 610a	SM.75, SM.82
	146o Gruppo T	603a, 609a	SM.82
	147o Gruppo T	601a, 602a	SM.82
	148o Gruppo T	606a	G.12
	149o Gruppo T	607a, 608a	SM.82
	158 Gruppo d' Assalto	236a, 387a, 388a	CR.42
	160o Gruppo CT	375a, 393a, 394a	CR.42, G.50
	Battaglione Aviazione Sahariana	26a, 99a	Ca.309, SM.81, SM.79, CR.42
		131a OA	Ca.311
		145a RM	Z.501, Z.506
		148a RM	G.12
		196a RM	Z.501
		600a T	Ca.133S
		614 Soccorso	Z.506s

The Italian Air Force in Africa had units for a variety of roles: fighter (CT: Caccia Terrestre), bomber (BT: Bombardamento Terrestre), army co operation / reconnaissance (OA: Osservazione Aerea), naval bomber (BM : Bombardamento Marittimo), ground attack / support (d' Assalto), dive bombing (BaT : Bombardamnento a Tuffo), torpedo plane (Aerosilurante), transport (T: Trasporto), naval reconnaissance (RM Ricognizione marittima), rescue (Soccorso). Additionally there was a group for the vast expanses of Libya (Gruppo Aviazione Presidio Coloniale) and a group for the oases in southern Libya (Battaglione Aviazione Sahariana).

ITALIAN AIRCRAFT TOTAL: 93 MC.202, 46 MC.200, 90 Fiat G.50, 45 Fiat CR.42, 25 Cant Z.1007, 24 Ca.311, 34 SM.79

Uniforms of the opposing forces in North Africa

The battle dress, as we know it today, came into being in the 1940s, specifically designed to fulfill the ergonomic requirements of modern-times war. Until then, any attempt to render any uniform more serviceable was frustrated by the set ideas and adherence to tradition characterizing the military commands in the European countries of the ancient regime. Even when the then great empires had to clothe their troops serving overseas with uniforms compatible with the conditions prevailing in tropical or subtropical regions; those uniforms, though made of lighter material, were patterned on the regular European ones and therefore were no more serviceable than before.

During World War II, when the conflict moved overseas, only a few countries were somewhat better prepared to face the scorching sun and the deserts, while others had little or no idea of what to expect.

Thanks to their colonies, Great Britain and France knew what to expect, though their progress in that respect had been minimal, since, at that time, tradition was bound to override necessity.

The Italians, relying for their patterns on the uniforms of the other colonial powers and drawing, perhaps, some inspiration from the clothing of the people of the Maghreb, tried to combine in their uniforms the classic elegance of the European ones with the relative comfort demanded by the climatic conditions.

The Germans, on the other hand, were driven, as early as July 1940, when their involvement in the Italian "adventure" in North Africa loomed large, to realize the necessity of providing their troops with tropical uniforms. To this end, the Tropical Research Institute of the University of Hamburg was assigned to prepare the relevant study, the results of which were immediately implemented. The Institute based its designs on the patterns of the uniforms worn by the German (until 1918) and British colonial troops.

In the illustrations that follow, one may acquire a clear idea not only of the resulting regulation battle dress, but also of the against-the-rules modifications it received along the way in order to be made more suitable to the climatic conditions prevailing in the area.

German troops advance to the El Alamein line. The Afrika Korps prepared for the battle knowing that it was at a distinct disadvantage. (Bundesarchiv)

AFRIKAKORPS

ARTILLERY 1st LIEUTENANT, DEUTSCHES AFRIKA KORPS. *(Oberleutnant der Artillerie, DAK) The M1940 tropical outfit includes field blouse (feldbluse), shirt, loose tie due to the heat and tropical breeches (all in olive green cotton fabric, typical of the 1941-1942 period army uniforms), with 1st pattern high lace-up boots made of leather and canvas. On his tropical cap (silver-piped for officers), beneath his antidust goggles, the red arm-of-service color (waffen-farbe) for the artillery, is denoted by inverted soutache chevron above the National cokcade, the shoulder straps underlay and the double-bar collar badges (Litzen M1935). All his badges are transferred from his temperate uniform. His decorations are the Iron Cross 1st Class and the General Assault badge. The Parabellum P08 hard leather pistol holster and the M1935 map case hang from the canvas. (standard issue for officers)*

1. INFANTRY CORPORAL, ROYAL ITALIAN ARMY. (Caporale di Fanteria, Regio Esercito Italiano)
Rank insignia as chevrons on the sleeves and the standard five-point "Star of Savoy" on the collar (still worn by all the members of the Italian Armed Forces today), the latter often appeared on the tropical dress lacking any underlay. Tropical jacket and trousers, similar in design to those of the European uniform, are shown here with M1907 ammunition pouches, M1891 waist belt, M1891 bayonet and scabbard from the European dress, in gray-green (brown leather equipment was standard for colonial troops), and Carcano M1891/1941 6.5mm rifle. The infantry emblem is stencil-painted black on the M1933 helmet overpainted sand-yellow.

2. MOTORISED TRANSPORT 1st LIEUTENANT, ROYAL ITALIAN ARMY. (Tenente di Motorizzata Transporti, Regio Esercito Italiano)
Lightweight tropical dress in one of the various earth/green color shade made from light cloth. The Sahariana tunic matches the breeches and the high "colonial" brown leather boots. The rank status is denoted by two white cast metal five-point stars, on each shoulder board and on the practical M1942 Bustina (envelope) side cap. The blue arm-of-service color of the Motorised Transport Corps is diaplayed on the rectangular collar badges and on the shoulder boards piping along the embroidered MTC emblem. The pistol holster is for a Beretta M1934.

1

2

1. MAJOR, ROYAL ARMOURED CORPS.
The only special features of the otherwise standard tropical dress is the black wool beret, the goggles and the holster for the .38
Enfield No2 Mk I revolver. His rank insignia, a Tudor crown embroidered on golden yellow underlay, is worn on light khaki
slip-on loops on both shoulder straps.

2. CORPORAL, AUSTRALIAN COMMONWEALTH MILITARY FORCES.
The uniforms and equipment of the Allied forces in North Africa were, for the most part, British. His equipment consists of an
SMLE No 1 Mk III rifle, M1907 bayonet, and water canteen. A Mk I helmet hangs on the 1937 Pattern web equipment waist
belt. The characteristic canvas gaiters and Australian slouch hat are the only evidence of this soldier's origin. The two
chevrons denoting his rank of corporal are shown on the right sleeve.

1. AIR FORCE SIGNALER. *(Funker Flieger der Luftwaffe)*
All Luftwaffe personnel were supplied with uniforms such as illustrated from 1941 onward. They differed from the army's (as was initially issued to the Luftwaffe) both in their colors, as well as in their design. The air force private has the typical web equipment of infantrymen. The soft blue-gray detachable shoulder straps are from the European field jacket and have the lemon yellow signals' waffenfarbe piping. The antidust goggles are Zeiss Umbral with blue-gray leather and detachable orange-red lenses.

2. LUFTWAFFE MAJOR. *(Major der Luftwaffe)*
A combination of elegance and practical design, with removable items (for example the white cover on the summer standard peaked cap, the shoulder straps, or the shirt buttons) Nevertheless, this major, buttoned up, proudly displays the Knight's Cross to his Iron Cross. The yellow arm-of-service color (waffen-farbe) on the shoulder straps indicates the flight personnel. The Nitsche & Gunter flying goggles were also useful on the ground during a sandstorm. There is a hand compass on the SWp 734 10-30 life jacket and a Walther P38 pistol on the waist belt. He is holding a throat-phones set and his oxygen supply hose and his flying helmet. (a Netzkopfhaube LKpN101 by Siemens, a mesh/net that varied in color shade from earth to chocolate made of cloth and chamois leather)

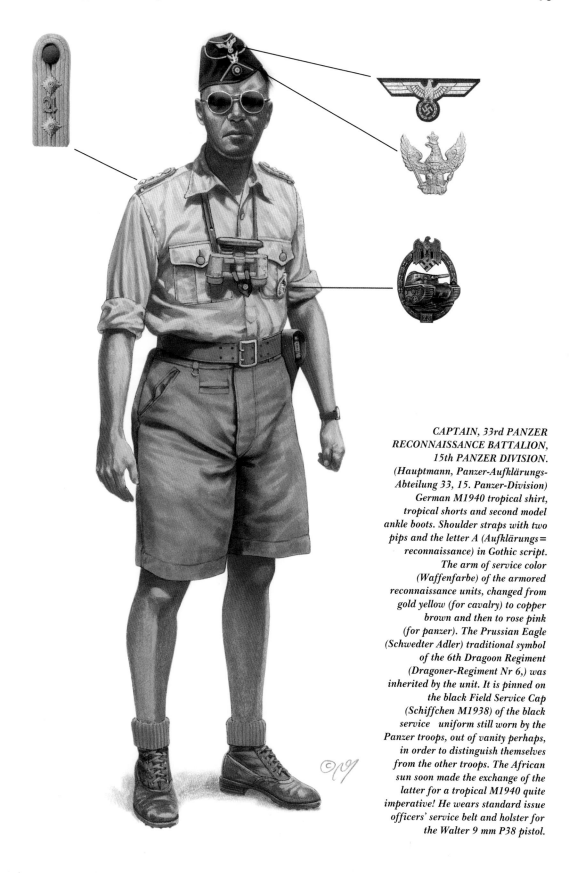

CAPTAIN, 33rd PANZER RECONNAISSANCE BATTALION, 15th PANZER DIVISION. *(Hauptmann, Panzer-Aufklärungs-Abteilung 33, 15. Panzer-Division) German M1940 tropical shirt, tropical shorts and second model ankle boots. Shoulder straps with two pips and the letter A (Aufklärungs= reconnaissance) in Gothic script. The arm of service color (Waffenfarbe) of the armored reconnaissance units, changed from gold yellow (for cavalry) to copper brown and then to rose pink (for panzer). The Prussian Eagle (Schwedter Adler) traditional symbol of the 6th Dragoon Regiment (Dragoner-Regiment Nr 6,) was inherited by the unit. It is pinned on the black Field Service Cap (Schiffchen M1938) of the black service uniform still worn by the Panzer troops, out of vanity perhaps, in order to distinguish themselves from the other troops. The African sun soon made the exchange of the latter for a tropical M1940 quite imperative! He wears standard issue officers' service belt and holster for the Walter 9 mm P38 pistol.*

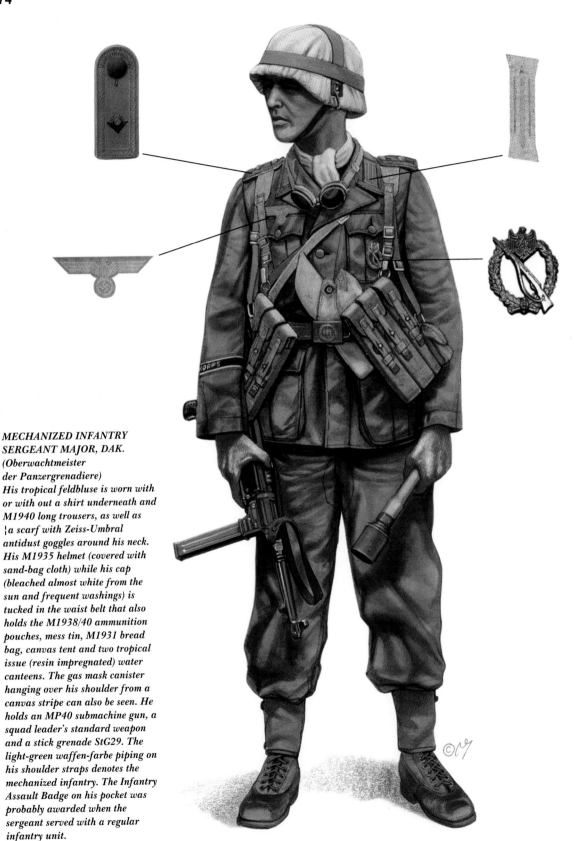

**MECHANIZED INFANTRY
SERGEANT MAJOR, DAK.**
*(Oberwachtmeister
der Panzergrenadiere)
His tropical feldbluse is worn with
or with out a shirt underneath and
M1940 long trousers, as well as
¦a scarf with Zeiss-Umbral
antidust goggles around his neck.
His M1935 helmet (covered with
sand-bag cloth) while his cap
(bleached almost white from the
sun and frequent washings) is
tucked in the waist belt that also
holds the M1938/40 ammunition
pouches, mess tin, M1931 bread
bag, canvas tent and two tropical
issue (resin impregnated) water
canteens. The gas mask canister
hanging over his shoulder from a
canvas stripe can also be seen. He
holds an MP40 submachine gun, a
squad leader's standard weapon
and a stick grenade StG29. The
light-green waffen-farbe piping on
his shoulder straps denotes the
mechanized infantry. The Infantry
Assault Badge on his pocket was
probably awarded when the
sergeant served with a regular
infantry unit.*

INFANTRY LANCE-CORPORAL, MACHINE GUN COMPANY.
(Gefreiter, Maschinengewehr-Kompanie)
The machine gunners in the German Army, usually held the rank of Corporal or Private 1st Class. Tropical web equipment consists of service belt and Y straps, a hardshell pistol leather holster for the Parabellum P 08, a cleaning and spare parts case to his MG 34 machine gun, M1931 water canteen and haversack, while a gas mask canister hangs from his shoulder. His No 2 would carry the machine gun's replacement barrels, ammunition and the tripod. The Gefreiter wears the heavy wool greatcoat with tropical-style rank chevrons on his left upper arm only, trousers fastened around the first model ankle boots. Common practice was the field gray (feldgrau) M1935 steel helmets, to be overpainted by the troops in the frontline in olive or ochre colors of various shades which were used for painting vehicles (often mixed with sand to give it a rougher appearance). The "Eagle" was unofficially replaced with the Afrikakorps "palm tree." Mud, too, was a rough solution for camouflage and insulation from the blazing sun, as were various covers, mostly pieces of sandbag cloth.

PARATROOPER, "RAMCKE" BRIGADE. *(Fallschirmjäger, Fallschirmjägerbrigade Ramcke) This battle dress incorporates several innovations. The "Meyer" cap (from Göring's nickname, "Hermann Meyer") with neck protection and the field blouse were originally intended for the Luftwaffe Division "Hermann Göring," but they became very popular and were widely adopted. The "Ramcke" tunic is a modification of the standard tropical Luftwaffe jacket, with breast pockets removed and flap openings added, used to secure the pouches or the machine gun ammunition belts during a jump by two vertical press stud sets. He is equipped with the 2nd pattern rubber-soled front lace-up jump boots. Sock (and gloves) sizes for the Wehrmacht are indicated by the means of white stripes, one, two and three for small, medium and large respectively. Also seen is his M1937 parachutist's helmet over-painted "sand yellow" and the M1884/89 bayonet scabbard, for his KAR 98k Mauser rifle, hanging from the waist belt.*

**FLYING OFFICER,
ROYAL AIR FORCE.**
*This fighter pilot is another
mixed dress example of tropical
shirt, civilian scarf, V-neck
sweater, Battle Dress blouse,
shorts, and shoes with long socks.
His pilot's wings are sewn on his
left breast, while his rank, that of
flying officer, are slip-on loops on
the shoulder straps. A Type-D
flying helmet, Type-E
microphone/oxygen mask, Mk Va
flying goggles, chamois gloves,
and seat-type parachute complete
the ensemble.*

**SECOND LIEUTENANT,
1st GREEK INFANTRY
BRIGADE.**
*(Anthypolokhagós)
Irregularities in this
fighting Greek's appearance
are justified by the extreme
weather conditions
encountered in the desert.
The tropical shirt and
trousers, V-neck khaki
sweater, greatcoat, other
ranks' black leather boots,
and gaiters are British
surplus (Army and/or
Air Force). The light khaki
summer service peaked cap
is Greek. His rank insignia,
a six-point star embroidered
(in white or aluminium
wire) on light khaki slip-on
loops is worn on both
shoulder straps.*

Tank forces in the Battle of El Alamein

Allied forces

The Allies entered World War II with the formation of their tank forces based on the obsolete concept of developing specialized tank types for each basic mission. This, in general, meant that specific tank types undertook the task of supporting advancing infantry, while light tanks were for fast, surprise attacks (and to exploit any breach in the enemy line) and reconnaissance. In essence, those tasks previously performed by the cavalry. A perfect example of this concept was the British tank forces that played the most decisive role during the Battle of El Alamein.

The British entered World War II persisting in retaining three different types of tank, each of which had some

The Battle of El Alamein was the decisive turning point of operations on the North African front. Careful study of the combatants' tank forces is imperative, as tanks played a crucial role in the confrontation. It is no overstatement to assert that the quantitative and qualitative superiority of the Allied armored forces were paramount in the victorious outcome of this vitally important battle.

special design characteristics relevant to a specific type of mission. First, there were the "light" tanks, which were used almost exclusively for reconnaissance, given that their armament and thin armor protection rendered them unfit for anything else.

A German Panzerjäger I tank destroyer. Twenty-seven of these vehicles arrived in Tripoli, Libya, in March 1941 with the 605th Tank Destroyer Battalion (Panzerjäger-Abteilung), and served throughout the North African operations until May 1943. The vehicle is based on the PzKpfw I light tank, with an armored superstructure and the Czech vz 38 47 mm anti-tank gun, one of the most efficient anti-tank guns at the beginning of the war.

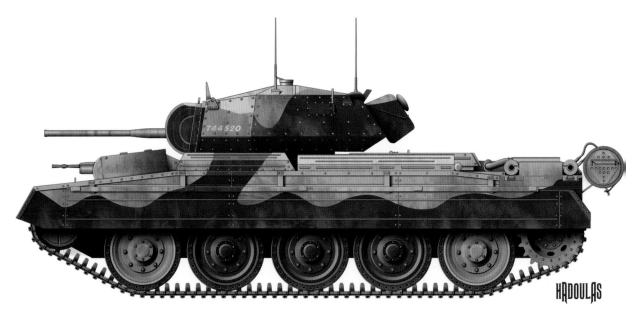

A Crusader Mk II tank of the 9th Lancers, 1st Armoured Division. Crusader crews did not fight so well in the First Battle of El Alamein, knowing their tank's weaknesses. Painted in standard light stone and dark green. The rhinoceros is the 1st Armoured Division's insignia and is painted on the tank's front fender. (Illustration by Dimitris Hadoulas/Historical Notes by Stelios Demiras)

The Grant Mk I was the first American medium tank to be received by the British forces. Its arrival reinforced the 8th Army's tank force, giving the British a tank with a 75mm gun and the ability to stop the German panzers. Its primary weakness was the placement of the main armament on the tank's right side, which greatly limited its field of fire. In addition, it had a high profile, making it a perfect target for German tanks and anti-tank guns. This one was assigned to "B" Squadron, 3rd Royal Tank Regiment, 8th Armoured Brigade, 10th Armoured Division (El Alamein, October 1942). Finished in light stone. Yellow rectangle on turret reveals that the tank was assigned to "B" Squadron. (Illustration by Dimitris Hadoulas/Historical Notes by Stelios Demiras)

Crusader and Sherman tanks advance at El Alamein.

The second category comprised the so-called "cruiser" tanks, which were tasked to carry out fast attacks, taking over the role previously carried out by the cavalry. Tanks in this category were also lightly armored to keep their weight low in order to fulfill this role, which demanded relatively high speed across all terrain types and, in general, a high rate of mobility. Finally, there were the "infantry" tanks, which were used exclusively in the support of the infantry in its advance by eliminating machine gun nests and other defensive positions. For this reason, they were heavily armored (for their time) at the expense of speed, which was, anyway, not an important factor as their speed only had to be adequate for them to cooperate with the infantry units.

In the three years from the beginning of World War II to the Battle of El Alamein, British opinion eventually underwent a profound change as a result of the experience gained from using armored forces on the modern battlefield. It was realized that this "division of labor" between the different tank categories was a theoretical concept that had little in common with reality. To be precise, light tanks, which had performed inadequately in every sphere, were completely driven from the battlefield and their use confined to reconnaissance duties, with any further development virtually halted in 1941. Meanwhile, cruiser tanks were given thicker armor protection

(their weakest point) and heavier armament, beginning with the Crusader I and II. However, their inbred design limitations did not allow for radical changes. This was only made possible with the introduction into service of new types of cruiser tanks, characterized perhaps by the A34 Comet of 1944, which was born through the experience gained by British tankers and their unequal battles with the German PzKpfw III and IV when equipped with their earlier cruiser tank model. As for the infantry tanks, they were equipped with heavier main armament (e.g., Churchill III), while more powerful engines improved their mobility.

The armored division, having undergone an organizational change in mid-1942, consisted basically of just one armored brigade and one motorized infantry brigade. The latter had replaced the second armored brigade the division had in its original form. Divisional units advanced on a broad front, followed by two infantry

Matilda Scorpion Mk. I flail tank. Based on the older Matilda Mk. II infantry tank that had operated successfully and extensively on the North African front during the initial stages of operations. All 12 tanks of this type that were engaged at El Alamein were assigned to the 1st Army Tank Brigade (42 and 44 Royal Tank Regiment).

A British 9th Royal Tank Regiment Valentine tank in the desert.

The interior of a PzKpfw III Ausf. J turret showing the loader and gunner's positions.

brigades belonging to another formation. This dualism quickly proved at the start of operations against the Germans in North Africa, to be a source of danger, and it weakened cooperation between the infantry and the tanks. The new, more balanced armored division organizational table eliminated these defects, giving a primary role to the combined advance of tanks and mechanized infantry, following, in many ways, German tactical thinking with their armored divisions. Its adoption was connected with the change of thought in British circles about the dispersal of forces. A similar

organizational change followed in British infantry divisions. Tank brigades, having been the primary infantry support units, were initially organic to the infantry divisions. However, it was soon realized that this was instrumental in weakening the infantry divisions by depriving them of the crucially important third infantry brigade when in their main element. The result was that this organizational scheme was also abandoned, with tank brigades once again being reconstituted as Army-level units that were attached to infantry formations if and when the need arose.

This did not apply to all armored formations, and out of the three armored divisions that took part in the Battle of El Alamein, the 7th and 10th had two armored brigades (4th, 22nd and 8th, 24th, respectively). Each armored brigade consisted of three armored regiments (battalions) and one motorized infantry battalion. The organization of the armored regiments did not change throughout the North African operations. Each consisted of three squadrons, plus a headquarters squadron and a reconnaissance troop that was organic to the headquarters squadron. Each squadron was made up of four troops (each with three or four tanks) and a squadron headquarters troop (usually of three tanks.)

The main armament equipping British design tanks during the Battle of El Alamein remained the 2-pdr (40 mm) gun, which was a 1930s design, when any tank's maximum armor thickness rarely exceeded 15-25 mm. However, by the time it entered service in 1936, rapid progress quickly revealed its inadequacies, although it remained in production until the beginning of 1942. It was replaced by no other than the famous 6-pdr (57 mm) gun, with

The M4A1 Sherman was the classic American tank of World War II and was used extensively by the Allied forces and mostly by the British after being received as American military aid. This is an initial production M4A1 of the 9th Lancers (The Bays), 2nd Armoured Brigade, 1st Armoured Division, 8th Army. It took part in the Battle of El Alamein. Finished in light stone, camouflaged in dark green. The rhinoceros badge is the 1st Armoured Division insignia. (Illustration by Dimitris Hadoulas/Historical Notes by Stelios Demiras)

An M3 Stuart I ("Honey") light tank of the British 7th Armoured Division, North Africa, 1942. It was the first American tank used by the British Army in World War II. The British received the M3's in June 1941 under the Lend-Lease program and named it "General Stuart." The tank's ability to shoot and move together with its highly reliable engine and the absolute reluctance to throw off its tracks led the British tank crews to nickname it "Honey." The 37 mm M6 gun proved adequate early in the North African Campaign, but by early 1942, the tank was outgunned by its German counterparts. After this, the tank was relegated to scouting and reconnaissance operations. This Stuart has sky-blue and brown stripes painted over the basic color of light stone. (Illustration by Dimitris Hadoulas/Historical Notes by Stelios Demiras)

its manifestly higher performance, which was fitted to the Crusader Mk III and Churchill Mk III tanks (84 in total) during the Battle of El Alamein.

An even more important influence on the outcome of the confrontation (apart from the overwhelming allied superiority) was the entering into service of the M3 Lee/Grant and M4 Sherman American tanks with the 8th Army's tank forces. These were characterized by the wonderful reliability of the engine/transmission components, a factor that was missing from British tanks. Both these tanks were equipped with a 75 mm main gun, which had good anti-tank performance and could also fire high explosive (HE) rounds. This latter factor finally gave the British tank crews equality when facing German anti-tank gun units, something that had been impossible in the past as British tanks lacked HE rounds. In the final analysis, adopting the principles of force concentration and combined operations decisively contributed to the outcome of the confrontation.

British M3 Grant of the 3rd Royal Tank Regiment is replenished with water before the battle.

A German mobile workshop abandoned in the desert.

Axis forces

In contrast to other combatants, most notably the British, who developed three different types of tank, each for a specific role, the Germans concentrated their efforts into designing tanks suitable for almost all operational requirements. As they had no preconceived ideas or outmoded misconceptions about the role of the new weapon, they approached the design challenges with an open mind, applying a rational program when forming their tank forces, and this was quickly made apparent from the first days of World War II. This program made provision for the manufacture, as a first phase, of a large number of light tanks that would form the nucleus of the Third Reich's future armored forces.

These tanks, the Panzerkampfwagen I and II, although remarkable designs, did not particularly distinguish themselves in any task. However, they were cheap to manufacture and became the tool with which the German tactics in the use of armored forces were formed and brought into

This PzKpfw III Ausf G of the 1st Company, PzRgt 8, 15th Panzer Division, was equipped with the wider 400 mm tracks that had first been fitted to late-production Ausf G's. The vehicle was painted overall Yellow/Brown desert camouflage with the turret number in red outlined white.

88 mm Flak 18 fires at British tanks. The German anti-tank guns played a dominant role in the North African conflict. The dual-role 88 mm gun was, without doubt, the most feared anti-tank gun by British tank crews.

CONCISE ORDER OF BATTLE OF OPPOSING FORCES			
8th Army		X Corps	1st Armoured Division
			10th Armoured Division
		XIII Corps	7th Armoured Division
			44th Infantry Division
			50th Infantry Division
		XXX Corps	51st (Highland) Division
			2nd New Zealand Division
			9th Australian Division
			4th Indian Division
			1st South African Division
Panzer Army Africa	German forces	Deutsches Afrika Korps (DAK)	19th Flak Division
			15th Panzer Division
			21st Panzer Division
			90th Light Division
			164th Light Division
	Italian forces	X Corps	"Brescia" Division
			"Folgore" Division
			"Pavia" Division
		XX Corps	"Ariete" Armored Division
			"Littorio" Armored Division
			"Trieste" Mechanized Division
		XXI Corps	"Trento" Division
			"Bologna" Division

Italian M13/40 tanks. Their light armor, inadequate armament, engine, and suspension (outdated Vickers type) did not work well in the desert environment, and they were very unreliable.

perfection. They were used extensively during the first two years of the war and in the initial stages of the North African operations. Neither of these tanks took part in the Battle of El Alamein. It should, perhaps, be noted that overcoming the difficulties encountered during the initial manufacturing process of the heavier Panzerkampfwagen III and Panzerkampfwagen IV was greatly helped by the know-how accumulated during the production of these light tanks. These latter two tanks were to become the mainstay of the German armored forces throughout World War II.

The Panzer division (Panzer-Division) was a Blitzkrieg (lightneing war) weapon. In its classic form (1935-1940), it consisted of one armored and one mechanized infantry brigade. The spectacular successes of German armored forces during the first two years of the war was the most decisive element influencing the outcome of land warfare, so it was decided to increase their number. This was to be achieved through the reduction of the number of tank units in each panzer division while, correspondingly, increasing the number of its infantry units. So, by the close of 1940, each panzer division was composed of one armored regiment

The Panzer IVAusf F2 with the long 75 mm gun was superior to any Allied tank during the Battle of El Alamein. However, Rommel only possessed a few, especially toward the end of the battle. This tank is assigned to the 8th Company, 2nd Battalion, 8th Panzer Regiment, 15th Panzer Division. It is finished in Desert Yellow. Visible on the turret is the number "8" denoting the company, the DAK insignia (white palm tree and swastika) and the 15th Panzer Division insignia (triangle divided by a vertical bar). Usual German practise was for tanks to have three digits on the turret, but this division adopted just one digit. *(Illustration by Dimitris Hadoulas/Historical Notes by Stelios Demiras)*

A German Afrika Korps 47 mm PaK(t) auf PzKpfw I Ausf B, Panzerjager Abteilung 605, El Alamein, November 1942. It was armed with the Skoda 47mm cannon KPUV. This Czech-designed weapon, designated Vz38 Model A5 anti-tank gun, had proved very effective during the initial stages of World War II. Around 27 of these self-propelled anti-tank guns arrived in Tripoli in March 1941 and saw service throughout the North African campaign right up until the capitulation in May 1943. The majority of them were painted sand yellow (RAL 8000) over their original dark gray (RAL 7021) base camouflage color. (Illustration by Dimitris Hadoulas/Historical Notes by Stelios Demiras)

MUZZLE VELOCITY AND ARMOR PENETRATION DATA OF OPPOSING TANKS (On thin homogeneous hard armor, angle of fall 30 degrees)			
GUN TYPE	MUZZLE VELOCITY	PENETRATION AT 500 M	PENETRATION AT 1000 M
2-pdr (40 mm) (British)	854 m/sec	50 mm	42 mm
6-pdr (57 mm) (British)	853 m/sec	81 mm	74 mm
M6 (37 mm) (American)	860 m/sec	50 mm	42 mm
M2 (75 mm) (American)	567 m/sec	60 mm	38 mm
M3 (75 mm) (American)	701 m/sec	70 mm	60 mm
KwK 38 L/42 (50 mm) (German)	685 m/sec	49 mm	36 mm
KwK 39 L/60 (50 mm) (German)	835 m/sec	60 mm	44 mm
KwK 37 L/24 (75 mm) (German)	385 m/sec	41 mm	35 mm
KwK 40 L/42 (75 mm) (German)	740 m/sec	91 mm	82 mm
M39 (47 mm) (Italian)	630 m/sec	42 mm	30 mm

A PzKpfw II of the 8th company, II Battalion, PzRgt 8, 15th Panzer Division, in Libya, 1941. The "8" is black and white, the division sign red, and the DAK palm trees white. The vehicle color is overall Yellow-Brown. (Bundesarchiv)

(Panzer – Regiment), two mechanized infantry regiments (Schützen, later Panzergrenadier – Regiment) mounted on armored personnel carriers or trucks, one reconnaissance battalion (Aufklärungsabteilung) mounted on armored vehicles and half-tracks, one artillery regiment (Artillerieregiment), one anti-tank artillery battalion (Panzerjägerabteilung), one anti-aircraft artillery battalion (Flak-Bataillon), one engineer battalion (Pionier-Bataillon), and one signals battalion (Nachrichtenabteilung). Each armored regiment had two, sometimes three armored battalions (Panzerabteilung), each of which had three tank companies (Panzer-Kompanie). From 1942, the tank companies were increased by one, so that each of the four companies had 22 tanks. Therefore, in theory, each German panzer division consisted of 164 tanks. A panzer division's smallest tactical unit was the tank troop (Panzerzug) equipped with four or five tanks.

From 1941, when the organizational changes had been completed, until the Battle of El Alamein, the German panzer divisions were equipped with, mostly, the PzKpfw III and PzKpfw IV, with the lighter PzKpfw I and IIs being demoted for use as reconnaissance tanks. Initially, each tank battalion

TECHNICAL CHARACTERISTICS OF ALLIED TANKS IN THE BATTLE OF EL ALAMEIN

TYPE	WEIGHT	MAXIMUM ARMOR THICKNESS	ENGINE	MAXIMUM SPEED	ARMAMENT	CREW
Crusader Mk. I/II (217 units)	19.2 t	40 mm	1 petrol Nuffield Liberty L-12 petrol 340 hp	43 km/h	1 QF 2-pdr gun, 2 Besa 7.92 mm machine guns	5
Crusader Mk. III (78 units)	19.2 t	49 mm	1 petrol Nuffield Liberty L-12 petrol 340 hp	43 km/h	1 QF 6-pdr gun, 2 Besa 7.92 mm machine guns	4
Valentine Mk. III (194 units)	16.2 t	65 mm	1 AEC A190 diesel 131 hp	24 km/h	1 QF 2-pdr gun, 1 Besa 7.92 mm machine gun	4
Churchill Mk. III (6 units)	39.5 t	102 mm	Bedford twin-six petrol 350 hp	24.8 km/h	1 QF 6-pdr gun, 2 Besa 7.92 mm machine guns	5
M3 Stuart (119 units)	12.4 t	44.5 mm	1 Continental W-670 petrol 250 hp	58 km/h	1 M6 37 mm gun 4 Browning 0.30 in. machine guns	4
M3 Lee / Grant (175 tanks)	27.6 t	37 mm	1 Wright (Continental) R975 EC2 petrol 340 hp	42 km/h	1 M2 / M3 75 mm gun, 1 M6 37 mm gun, 4 Browning 0.30 in. machine guns	6
M4 Sherman (251 tanks)	31.5 t	77 mm	1 Continental R975 C1 petrol 400 hp	42 km/h	1 M3 75 mm gun 3 Browning 0.30 in. machine guns	5

TECHNICAL CHARACTERISTICS OF AXIS TANKS IN THE BATTLE OF EL ALAMEIN

TYPE	WEIGHT	MAXIMUM ARMOR THICKNESS	ENGINE	MAXIMUM SPEED	ARMAMENT	CREW
Panzerkampfwagen III Ausf G/H (85 units)	20.3 t/ 21.6 t	37 mm/ 37+30 mm	1 Maybach HL 120 TRM petrol 320 hp	40 km/h	1 KwK 38 L/42 50 mm gun, 2 MG 34 7.92 mm machine guns	5
Panzerkampfwagen III Ausf J/L (88 units)	21.6 t	50 mm/57 mm	1 Maybach HL 120 TRM petrol 320 hp	40 km/h	1 KwK 38 L/42 50 mm (J) / 1 KwK 39 L/60 50 mm (L), 2 MG 34 7.92 mm machine guns	5
Panzerkampfwagen IV Ausf E/F1 (8 units)	21 t / 22.3 t	30+30 mm/ 50 mm	1 Maybach HL 120 TRM petrol 320 hp	42 km/h	1 KwK 37 L/24 75 mm gun, 2 MG 34 7.92 mm machine guns	5
Panzerkampfwagen IV Ausf F2 (30 units)	23 t	50 mm	1 Maybach HL 120 TRM petrol 320 hp	40 km/h	1 KwK 40 L/43 75 mm gun, 2 MG 34 7.92 mm machine guns	5
Carro Armato M13/40 – M14/41 (278 units)	14 t/14.5 t	42 mm	1 SPA 8 TM 40 diesel 125 hp / 1 SPA 15 TM 41 diesel 145 hp	32 km/h	1 M39 47 mm gun, 2 Breda 8 mm machine guns	4

included two companies of PzKpfw IIIs and one of PzKpfw IVs. The PzKpfw IVs were used for fire support missions, as their early versions were equipped with the short-barreled 75 mm KwK 37 L/24. With the improvement of armor protection in the Allied camp, upgrading the main armament of German tanks became imperative. During this process, the larger PzKpfw IV proved to have more scope for development in this sector, so roles of the two tanks was reversed, with the PzKpfw IVs taking

over the role of dealing with enemy tanks and the PzKpfw IIIs giving fire support to the panzer division's tank regiment. Characterizing this change was that the final versions of the PzKpfw III (Ausf M and N) were equipped with the 75 mm KwK 37 L/24 gun, which had, initially, armed the PzKpfw IV.

As for Italian tanks, the basic type used during the Battle of El Alamein was the M13/40. It was a mechanically unreliable tank, technologically outdated, as were all Italian tanks of the period, with deficient performance across all fields. However, it was also the only tank of note the Italians possessed in sufficient numbers. When the M14/41 entered service, things did improve somewhat with respect to mobility as this tank was equipped with special sand filters and was more reliable.

The typical German panzer division was a totally balanced formation that possessed a clear offensive character. Its success lay in its

ability to apply tremendously strong pressure on a small sector of the enemy's lines. The panzer division, using its panzer regiment as the attack's spearhead and with Luftwaffe close support, concentrated its strength on a sector of the front no more than 4 kilometers wide, but usually less than 2 kilometers. The attack was launched with the tank force forming an armored wedge (keil), each side of which was tasked with dealing with specific sections of the enemy's defense. The firepower, and sheer impetus of the assault were, usually, enough to breach the enemy's line and to lead the attacking forces in sufficient depth beyond the front line. Other divisional units then quickly attacked through the breach in the enemy lines, predominantly mechanized infantry regiments (later called panzergrenadier), which neutralized isolated pockets of resistance that had been bypassed by the tanks and consolidated already overrun terrain.

One of the first tanks to reinforce the Deutsches Afrika Korps (DAK) in May 1942 was this Panzer III of 1st Company, 8th Panzer Regiment, 15th Panzer Division. Rommel had a mere 19 Panzer IIIs with the long 50 mm gun. It is finished in Desert Yellow. It sports the DAK insignia (white palm tree and swastika), 15th Panzer Division insignia (triangle divided with a vertical bar), and the vehicle number, 1 in this case, which is repeated on the rear of the turret, denoting 1st Company. (Illustration by Dimitris Hadoulas/Historical Notes by Stelios Demiras)

M 14/41, Italian 132nd Armored Division "Ariete." Because of its obsolete tanks, this formation suffered heavy casualties and had just a few operational tanks by the end of June when it took part in the First Battle of El Alamein. This tank is the second tank of the 1st Platoon, 3rd Company, and was finished in Sand Yellow (giallosabbia.) (Illustration by Dimitris Hadoulas/Historical Notes by Stelios Demiras)

This Horch s.E. Pkw, Kfz 69, has been converted into a self-propelled mount for a 20 mm Flak 38. The Yellow/Brown has been neatly sprayed over the entire vehicle, with a small area of original Dark Gray showing around the DAK palm. The Flak 38 is still in its original Dark Gray. The four-leaf clover is green on a white square. (Bundesarchiv)

Force concentration and continuous movement were the two cornerstones of the tactics followed by the German panzer divisions. Force concentration was dictated by the tactical idea that considered that ensuring sufficient firepower was brought to bear on a particular sector of the front as a necessary prerequisite to achieve a breach in the enemy's defensive lines. Continuous movement was dictated by the fact that the enemy commander would not be able to cope with an agile, fast-moving force that constantly changed its positions, effectively and on time, thus creating a fluid situation on the battlefield.

Following the outflanking movement, and the elimination of pockets of resistance, it was then necessary to create defense lines to counteract any possible enemy counterattack. The divisional anti-tank artillery battalion, always closely cooperating with the tanks, had the primary role in this phase of the attack. The tanks undertook to repulse the enemy if he counterattacked in a bid to recapture his initial positions. The German tank formations often adopted a mixture of offensive and defensive tactics, especially if repulsing an enemy attack proved difficult, seeking to lure the enemy tanks toward their anti-tank artillery positions, which then attempted to cause the maximum damage on the attackers, thus checking the enemy counterattack.

This Italian tankette, a CV35(L3) radio vehicle, is missing its antenna. It was part of "Ariete" Division and belonged to the company's 2nd platoon. The L3 tankette proved to be vulnerable to virtually all British tanks and armored cars. Even armor-piercing bullets were capable of penetrating many of the "armor" plates. It was designed as a reconnaissance vehicle, but wartime conditions forced the Italians to use it as a light tank, with poor results. (Bundesarchiv)

A command tank (PzKpfw III) of the 1st Battalion, PzRgt 8, displays an interesting variant of the 15th Panzer Division sign: While the symbol is in the vehicle color, the surrounding circular field is red. The "I" is also red, on a yellow-brown vehicle. (Bundesarchiv)

British tank crews were unlucky enough to have been on the receiving end of this tactic many times during operations in North Africa. The effectiveness of German anti-tank artillery was especially notable throughout the operations in this theater. This success was not only due to the exceptionally fine equipment possessed by the Germans, including guns, aiming devices, and ammunition, but also to the high level of troop training, without which the efficient use of the equipment would have been impossible.

Finally, it should not be forgotten that the application of the principles of high mobility (as well as general tactical flexibility) would not have been possible without taking into account the fact that, from the onset of the war, all German tanks were equipped with

A close-up of the right front side of a German PzKpfw III Ausf L tank. Note the round MG 34 7.92 mm machine gun mantlet ("Kugelblitz" type) and the additional 20 mm armor on the front glacis.

both radios and intercom. Command was exercised, in contrast to the British army, primarily through oral and not written orders, and local commanders were left with broad powers to act under their own initiative as, without doubt, they possessed a better picture of the tactical situation at that moment.

After the battle

After a battle lasting many days, such as the Battle of El Alamein, it is natural to follow the route, strewn with destroyed tanks, vehicles and the dead of a retreating army. However, on this occasion, reality was different.

"On the 3rd November, we knew the enemy had been beaten, as air force reports started arriving, revealing that the retreat was underway. We also knew that Rommel did not have enough transport to carry the majority of his forces. However, on the 3rd November we were not yet in open country, as the enemy continued blocking the passes with anti-tank weapons. However, the 51st Division and 4th Indian Division traversed these points, following a

The Greek Military Cemetery at El Alamein.

successful surprise attack on the night of the 3rd November. We had won the battle in 11 days, which was also the Army Commander's estimate for how long this great battle would take. The enemy had been beaten and was in retreat, while our armor was now operating in wide, open country.

"We had hoped that the air force would cause enormous damage to the enemy's transport as soon as the first signs that he was retreating were observed. These first reports talked about vehicles moving west, with traffic jams building up with four, sometimes, eight vehicles abreast, on and off the road. However, the results were very disappointing. As we followed the road from the battlefield of El Alamein towards Daba, I expected to see a scene of desolation, but there were very few destroyed vehicles. It is a fact that, at this juncture in the war, we had not yet

practiced low-level strafing attacks, as our fighter-bombers were used primarily for dog fighting and bombing missions. My belief is that air attacks on the retreating enemy were mostly carried out through comparatively high-level bombing, as our pilots were forbidden to fly at low level. This is undoubtedly true, as Allied pilots had not been fully trained for low-level strafing attacks and so a chance of paralyzing the enemy's retreat was definitely lost. Also, another great disappointment was that we were unable to completely cut off Rommel's remaining forces. If we had done, it would have saved us the intense, endless series of operations that were see us drive to Tripoli and beyond.

The German Military Cemetery at El Alamein. Behind its imposing closed walls lie 4,200 German soldiers.

The British Commonwealth Military Cemetery, east of El Alamein. Here lie 7,367 fallen Allied soldiers from Britain, Australia, New Zealand, South Africa, Greece, France, and India.

Decades later there are still piles of live ammunition concentrated in restricted desert areas, where civilians are still not allowed.

"However, Montgomery was fully aware that it was just a matter of time. Moreover, he was certainly extremely unlucky, as our forces, which had been ordered to cut off the enemy at the Fuka escarpment and the Mersa Matruh pass, were unable to do so and, a little later, they were pinned down by torrential rains and storms while in pursuit of the retreating enemy."

- An excerpt from an after the battle report of El Alamein by Major

General Sir Francis de Guingand, Montgomery's Chief of Staff (1942 to 1945).

If Rommel held any hopes of once more reversing his luck against the 8th Army after the Battle of El Alamein, they were quickly dashed by the Allied landings on the morning of 8 November 1942, of more than 100,000 American and British troops in Morocco and Algeria that opened a second front in the German's rear. The Afrika Korps' sole chance of

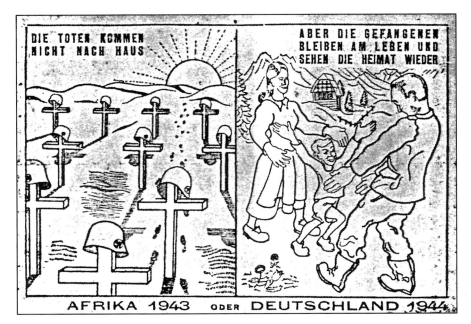

The Allies "bombed" the Germans with flyers, like the one in this photograph, a short time after the Battle of El Alamein urging them to surrender. At top left: "The dead do not return home," and, on the right: "but prisoners of war stay alive and soon return home."

survival then lay in a successful withdrawal to the Tunisian bridgehead. Rommel had been ill in Austria when the Battle of El Alamein began but flew to Africa immediately. After studying the situation, as it had been an overwhelming enemy attack, he decided to withdraw his army to the Fuka escarpment, 100 kilometers west of El Alamein. That would upset the balance of Montgomery's war machine. However, Rommel's intentions were not to be realized, as Hitler insisted that there be no withdrawal. In consequence, any withdrawal was merely delayed until the defeat on the battlefield. Even then, Rommel carried it out by showing the intelligence he was so well known for, coolly calculating that by abandoning his less mobile and experienced troops, including most of the Italian forces, he had a chance of retreating with his elite troops, using the means of transport and fuel at his disposal.

The opportunity of cutting him off had been lost, as the pursuit had been neither fast nor extensive enough in the Allied move to encircle him. First

British Humber armored reconnaissance vehicle.

of all, the British quickly captured most of the forces retreating along the coast road but lost valuable time. Farther to the west, they were unable, yet again, to cut off the German units in the Charing Cross area, close to Mersa Matruh and 190 kilometers west of El Alamein, due to a fuel shortage caused by the torrential rains. The rain zone could have been avoided with a wider encircling move by driving deeper into the country's interior.

When Rommel finally escaped the "jaws" of the Allied armored pursuit, he only halted when he had reached the defensive position of his own choice, close to El Agheila, at the other end of Cyrenaica, 1,130 kilometers west of El Alamein. He managed to escape his pursuers by going on a 15-day high-speed retreat, leaving behind just a few prisoners of war, mostly Italians and supplies.

The rough, inhospitable desert of North Africa, where sand, stones, and rocks alternate with huge sand dunes, was a battlefield and the area from which the German forces dramatically retreated.

The Daring Escape Of The Ramcke Parachute Brigade

Brigadier General Ramcke's airborne unit, consisting of four parachute battalions (Fallschirmjäger-Bataillon), one anti-tank company (Panzerjäger-Kompanie), and one engineer company (Pionier-Kompanie), was formed to take part in the planned invasion of Malta. The brigade moved first to Greece and then, in August 1942, to Libya due to the worsening situation. Its first battalion, under Major Groh, arrived in Africa on 4 August, the second, under Major von der Heydte, on the 10th August, and the third, under Major Hubner, in the evening of 17 August. Its fourth battalion was Battalion Burkhardt (a demonstration/training (Lehr) Battalion.) The brigade was officially placed under the command of the

One of the participants of the Battle of El Alamein in London's Imperial War Museum, the British MkII Matilda infantry tank. It carried 78 mm-thick armor plate, but its 2-pdr gun was not powerful enough to cause much damage to the German panzers unless from comparatively close range. Finished in the characteristic desert scheme. (dazzle pattern)

British Mk III Crusader tank.

Afrika Korps on 15 August 1942. The Brigade forces possessed very few vehicles as they had been transported to Libya by air. So, the 135th Anti-Aircraft Artillery Regiment (Flak-Regiment 135) loaned some of its vehicles to carry the paratroopers to the front, with very few of these vehicles being later permanently assigned to the brigade. In view of the impending British attack, they were almost immediately moved to El Alamein, where they were positioned in the front's central sector between the Italian "Trento" Division and the Italian X Corps. The tough paratroopers, after fighting stubbornly, retained their positions throughout the battle but had to share the fate of the remainder of the Afrika Korps units, moving on foot when the German forces began the retreat. This they had to do through the desert, with very little mechanized transport and carrying all of their supplies. However, they had an enemy in their rear that seemed to hesitate in pursuing them; he was even trying, at times, to clear lanes through the numerous minefields while being harassed by German artillery fire covering the retreat.

American M3 Grant medium tank, used in great numbers by the British Army during the battles in the desert.

Reports filtering into Rommel's headquarters stated that the Italian X Corps forces had quickly been surrounded by the British and almost all the troops had been captured. Rommel's German staff officers had also concluded that the troops of Ramcke's Brigade had met the same fate. Reality, however, was different. The paratroopers had already been marching northwest in an attempt to regain contact with the main body of the German forces, having lost contact with the rest of the Afrika Korps from the day the retreat started. They soon realized that the British armor, which was closely pursuing the German

Generaloberst von Arnim sagt euch :

« VOR UNS DER FEIND ! »
« HINTER UNS DIE SEE ? »

« ES GIBT KEIN ZURUECK MEHR ! »

EUER VERSTAND SAGT EUCH :

« HINTER DEM FEIND : DAS SAMMELLAGE
« HINTER DEM SAMMELLAGER : DAS
GEFANGENENLAGER IN ENGLAND ODER AMER
« HINTER DEM GEFANGENENLAGER :
HEIMAT ! »

« ES GIBT EIN ZURUECK

Another Allied propaganda flyer utilizing von Arnim's orders, one of Rommel's generals. On one side are his orders with the propagandists' comments on the other. On the front it reads: "Lieutenant General von Arnim informs you: 'In front of us is the enemy. Behind us is the sea. There is no room for retreat!'" Overleaf it reads: "Your logic says: "Behind the enemy is the prisoner of war camp. Behind the prisoner of war camp: prisoners of war in England or America. Behind the prisoners of war camp: Homeland' There is a way to return home!"

A German 50 mm Pak 38 anti-tank gun.

mechanized units, had already bypassed them and was to their west, so they had to move a lot more carefully.

A little before nightfall on 6 November, Ramcke's men noticed a British supply column that had halted for the night a few kilometers before Fuka. A raiding party was immediately organized, and the men approached the British vehicles, crawling in silence. The paratroopers neutralized the guards and the few drivers and were soon in possession of the vehicles, without a shot being fired. It was a supply convoy for a British armored unit, a pleasant surprise for the hungry, tired Germans who discovered priceless supplies like water, food, cigarettes, and, naturally, plenty of fuel. So, a few hours later, without encountering any further problems, the fully "mechanized" Ramcke Brigade rejoined Rommel's retreating army.

From 3 November, the brigade paratroopers had covered 325 kilometers, retreating across the desert, mostly on foot. Soon after, the

Two armored towers used for guard duties just once during the war in the desert. They are at the entrance to the Egyptian War Museum at El Alamein.

brigade was sent to the rear for a few days of hard-earned rest. Ramcke, meanwhile, was ordered to report to Germany where, on 15 November 1942, he was awarded the Oak Leaves to the Knight's Cross, that he had already been awarded, for the remarkable achievement of leading his entire unit to safety, avoiding capture by the enemy.

What remains today from the battle of El Alamein?

Today, a visitor to the site of this great North African battle will be disappointed if he tries to locate any remains of the hundreds of tanks, armored vehicles, guns, and even aircraft that were destroyed and abandoned by both protagonists in the coastal area.

Hundreds of tons of abandoned materiel at El Alamein, like everywhere in North Africa where battles had been fought, was collected during the following decades after the war ended. The majority of it was turned into scrap metal. Naturally, if someone ventures south into the desert, toward, say, Ruweisat Ridge,

German 150 mm sFH8 towed howitzer.

he might be lucky enough to stumble across some rusty remains of vehicles or materiel, coils of barbed wire, and, almost certainly, ammunition abandoned from that war.

Today, El Alamein is a small dusty village on the road from Alexandria to Mersa Matruh. Efforts have been made by the Egyptian authorities to preserve its history, with a small war museum being built, collecting and displaying enough remains from the battle, mostly tanks, armored vehicles and guns in an open area, with no protection against the elements.

The most notable places to pay tribute to the fallen of the battle are, naturally enough, the area's military cemeteries. The British Military

English POWs await transportation away from the front lines. (Bundesarchiv)

Italian self-propelled assault gun, Semovente M40 (75/18).

Cemetery lies east of El Alamein. Therein lie 7,367 Allied dead from Great Britain, Australia, New Zealand, Greece, France, and India.

The German and the Italian military cemeteries are also to the west of the area. In the imposing, enclosed walls of the German cemetery lie 4,200 German dead.

It goes without saying that these thousands of Allied, German, and Italian dead were collected and reburied in these cemeteries from the many different places across the battlefield where they had fallen and had been hastily buried. This epic battle was the turning point of the war in North Africa and, indeed, of World War II.

The participation of the 1st Greek Infantry Brigade at the Battle of El Alamein

The participation of the 1st Greek Infantry Brigade at the Battle of El Alamein in 1942 has special significance for Greece. Free Greek forces in Africa took part in a battle against the Axis forces, directly following the completion of the capture of Greece by the Axis. The brigade's battles were epic and won the admiration of all the Allies.

Two German divisions (15th Panzer and 5th Light) under General Rommel took part in operations on the North African front with the Italian forces from February 1941. These forces formed the German Afrika Korps (Deutsche Afrika Korps, DAK). Rommel initiated his operations against the Allies in May 1941 and was in Mersa Matruh by 25 June 1942. Then, on reaching El Alamein around the end of June, he halted his advance to Suez as his forces were completely exhausted and, additionally, he had received no reinforcements to replace his losses.

Greek troops of the 1st Greek Brigade attack German positions during the Battle of El Alamein. (Painting by Thanos Vasilikos)

The first battle between the Allied and Axis forces was held in the area of El Alamein from 1 to 27 July 1942, with it developing into four different phases. In that battle, General Auchinleck, the allied forces commander, was unable to achieve his goal of destroying Rommel's forces.

Auchinleck was replaced by General Montgomery, who led the 8th Army from El Alamein to Tunisia, literally crushing the enemy forces. This decisive battle of World War II lasted from 23 October to 13 November 1942.

Participation of the 1st Greek Infantry Brigade

The 1st Greek Infantry Brigade, which began its formation in Palestine and Syria from the end of June 1941, took part in the Battle of El Alamein that became the turning point of World War II. Its personnel consisted of Greek officers and men who had escaped from occupied Greece along with volunteers from the Middle East, mostly from Egypt. The brigade remained in Palestine at the Kfar Yona camp until May 1942. On 15 May, it relocated to Syria, where its training continued.

The brigade's composition was:
● Commander
● Staff and headquarters company
● Three infantry battalions
● Artillery regiment (battalion-sized)
● Reconnaissance company (armored cars)
● Engineer company
● Transport company
● Supply company
● Signals and military police detachments
● Workshop
● Field Dressing Station

While Infantry Colonel Evaggelos Antoniou was the brigade's first commanding officer, it was Infantry Colonel Pafsanias Katsotas who was in command during the actual period of operations (18 May 1942 to 24 March 1943).

The brigade is gradually sent forward into the area of operations

From the first months of 1942, the Greek Government in Cairo applied pressure on the British to use the Greek brigade in operations. Following a number of attempts, the British finally condoned the use of Greek Forces in the Middle East in Allied operations. So it was that, from the beginning of August 1942, the brigade was moved piecemeal from the Ras Baalbek camp in Syria to the Nile Delta, where it was placed under command of the headquarters of the forces defending the Nile Delta. It was then attached to the 50th Division, that had been assigned to the defense of the northern Delta area. The Brigade was placed in defensive positions in the area east of Amiriya.

Rommel's advance toward the Suez Canal was checked at the Battle of Alam Halfa (30 August to 2 September 1942) causing him to adopt a defensive posture. The brigade remained in its positions, east of Amiriya, throughout the Battle of Alam Halfa.

The Greek brigade in the front line

Following the 8th Army's orders to move up to the front line, the Greek brigade was reassigned to a higher formation and given a new mission. So from 9 September, the Brigade was moved through the desert by road to Alam Nayil, taking up a position in the southern sector of the front (in the XIII Corps area.)

The brigade remained in its defensive positions in this sector until the eve of the Allied attack (23 October 1942). Up until the eve of the attack on Al Alamein, its tasks were to improve the defenses and send reconnaissance patrols to collect information on the enemy's exact positions and order of battle. It was discovered that the 20th Italian Infantry Regiment, as well as German paratroopers, were beefing up the defenses facing the Brigade. On 12 October, the brigade was reassigned to the 50th British Division.

Due to an unprecedented sand storm, all work ceased in the brigade's sector around the middle of October. During that time, on 20 and 21 October, the brigade successfully sent patrols both into the interior and behind the German lines.

Plan of operations for the attack

According to the 8th Army Operations Plan, the 50th Division, under which it operated, assigned the brigade to the following missions, attack on a section of its choice, a raiding mission southeast of Point 104, harassment missions and being in readiness to repulse any enemy counterattack.

The brigade's participation in the attack

On the basis of 50th British Division operational orders, the brigade fulfilled the following missions:

● Attack against positions of an advanced enemy company on the night of 23 October.

● On 24 October, the brigade determinedly held its occupied positions.

● Company-strength attack against Point 104 on the night of the 25 October.

● General Montgomery ordered the brigade to replace the 8th Battalion, Durham Light Infantry (151st Brigade), that was on its left, following a regrouping plan that encompassed the entire 8th Army. The Brigade undertook defensive operations in its sector, harassing and deceiving the enemy with raiding missions and being ready for the all-out attack. During this phase of operations, the Brigade accomplished the following missions: It took over the 2nd Free French Brigade Group's positions in the area of the Brigade group's 3rd Battalion, that had advanced on the left on 26 October. On the night of 1 November, it successfully penetrated the enemy lines with a reinforced company. However, the front had been breached in the north and operations in the south followed in accordance with these developments. There were indications that the enemy was withdrawing.

In the meantime, from 1 November and following an order from 50th Division, the brigade was ordered to have patrols at readiness to be sent out to maintain contact with the enemy. In short, the brigade's main operational actions were: On the evening of 3 November, two mechanized brigade companies successfully pursued the enemy. Pursuit of the enemy continued on 4 November. It reinforced the battalion's attack on Point 103. During the night of 5 November, it isolated an Italian force and captured 314 prisoners. From 6 November, it took part in the continued pursuit of the enemy. By nightfall, its units had pushed forward to a depth of 30 kilometers. On 7 November it made contact with the 69th British Brigade. Until 13 November, the brigade was tasked with the job of collecting enemy matériel.

Brigade regrouping and moving to Aghedabia

On 14 November, under a new 8th Army order, the brigade was reassigned to the 44th British Division. Following the order, in the early morning of 15 November the brigade moved to its new position, which was in the area of Qeisan, south of El Alamein. It remained there until 28 November, regrouping and replacing its losses. On 29 November, it moved to another position and then, on 7 December, moved to Aghedabia.

Brigade's departure from the front

On 19 December, under orders from the commander-in-chief, the brigade left from the zone of operations and returned to Egypt.

Hoisting the Greek flag over a North African camp.

This order caused mixed reactions among the Greeks, as the foreign ministers of the three great powers (Great Britain, USA, and USSR) had made favorable statements about the fortunes of the Albanian people. Finally, the brigade moved to the area of Amiriya (close to the Nile Delta). So ended its participation in Allied operations that had begun on 8 September 1942.

Conclusions

The Allied victory at El Alamein held a special significance for Greece because of the 1st Greek Infantry Brigade's decisive contribution. The battles fought by the troops of the Brigade were equal to the epic battles fought two years earlier on the Northern Epirus front. The 1st Greek Infantry Brigade, by its courageous actions, added new pages of glory in the Greek military annals.

The brigade successfully completed all the missions assigned to it. This is evident from the reports by the higher formations and authorities concerning its actions at El Alamein. General Montgomery wrote, among others, in a personal letter to the brigade commander on 21 December 1942: "... The distinguished troops always and immediately fulfilled each mission assigned to them and their merit on the battlefield raised the deep respect of British Empire forces... ." The brigade sustained the following casualties, from its first deployment in the front line, during the Battle of El Alamein and the pursuit of the enemy: Six officers and 83 troops killed, 26 officers and 202 troops wounded.

Secret war in North Africa

The participants in the Battle of El Alamein, which ranked with the Battle of Stalingrad as one of the turning points of the war, were those not only present on the battlefield, but also away from it, and, as is true of all great battles, intelligence and spy warfare, played an important role.

The DAK made extensive use of motorcycles and motorcycle/sidecar combinations. The tactical sign on the sidecar of this one reveals it belonged to a towed artillery battery.

In all great military operations there are visible and invisible actors. The visible ones appropriate all the glory, not only because they are visible to the entire world, but because the invisible ones must remain obscure not only during the duration of the war but maybe for many years after it. One way to gain information about the enemy is to listen to his radio transmissions, without, of course, him knowing about it. This can be achieved by using electronic devices to listen to the enemy or by breaking his codes. This information can be gained a lot easier during wartime because there is a category of people, for example ignorant and/or inexperienced diplomats or diplomatic officials, or others, such as military or civilian personnel, who pay no attention to matters of security or by the old adage that "even walls have ears... . "

The battle in the North African desert between the Axis and British imperial troops was no exception to this eavesdropping game. Both sides exploited information gathered in this manner. The British gained a major advantage when they secured the standard German cipher machine, known as "Enigma." This secret was only revealed many years after the war, while the Germans and history were still attributing the information leak to Italian infidelity. What is interesting about this story is that the information obtained did not bring the results worthy of such an advantage on the battlefield. We will soon see why.

The first Enigma machine was built in 1923 by an engineer, Arthur Scherbius, and cost $144 U.S. dollars on the open market. The first machines could create 17,576 cipher alphabets, while later models created 456,976. This machine reached the British after a very strange trip around Europe.

A parcel for a German company arrived in Warsaw on a Saturday in January 1929. A company representative immediately rushed to customs and asked for the parcel to be returned to the sender as it contained radio components. The German haste made the Poles suspicious, so they delayed the parcel's return until the following Monday. Meanwhile, over the weekend, they opened the parcel and discovered an Enigma machine. After taking photos of it and after making sketches of its inner workings, it was repackaged and returned to Germany. No one in the Polish intelligence service paid any further attention to this machine until 1931, when Polish agents in Germany informed their superiors that the German army and navy were using a new cipher machine called Enigma. The Poles purchased such a machine on the open market and then compared it with the one they had studied two years before. The Germans paid no attention to the Poles buying such a machine, as it was useless without the codes used to send messages. In such a case, deciphering would take endless combinations until a meaning cropped up to enable them to convert a message in cipher into a clear text. Poles, on their part, assigned the breaking of Enigma to three of their best mathematicians, who were studying cryptanalysis at the University of Poznan. Finally, the Poles broke the German code and deciphered the first German message during the 1932 Christmas holidays. The Germans, in the meantime, had supplied the Enigma machine in thousands to all army, navy and air force units, as well as to their intelligence services.

The Poles had progressed their Enigma cryptanalysis by 1939, and, a

month before the German invasion of Poland, had informed and supplied the British and the French with Enigma material. What they did not know was that a mathematician and fellow countryman had already sold the Enigma machine secrets to the British secret services for £10,000, a British passport and permission for permanent residence for him and his wife in Paris. By that time, Britain had formed a unit called ULTRA (from Ultra Secret) at Bletchey Park, where all German signals enciphered with Enigma were intercepted and deciphered. ULTRA services proved invaluable and played their role in the North African operations. No British generals there capitalized more on the information from ULTRA than Field Marshal Montgomery before, during, and after the Battle of El Alamein.

The war in the Libyan and Egyptian desert see-sawed between Libya and Egypt before the Axis' final defeat. The two protagonists used any and all means available to obtain the enemy's secrets before the Battle of El Alamein. The Germans, as well as the British, had organized their intercept and deciphering services. The British had a direct access to German signals thanks to ULTRA, while the Germans, the Deutsches Afrika Korps to be precise, had indirect access to their enemy's signals thanks to the unintentional assistance of a neutral power...the Americans. The Germans had obtained an American code from their allies, the Italians, as the British had obtained Enigma secrets from their allies, the Poles. This code allowed Rommel to collect the most precise intelligence that any general could wish for about the enemy, thanks to the involuntary help of the American military attaché in Cairo, Brevet Colonel Bonner Frank Fellers (until, that is, July 1942).

During the early stages of the North African campaign, the 88 mm Flak 18, seen here behind an SdKfz 8 12-tonne tractor, was Rommel's "secret weapon." Designed as a dual-purpose weapon for both anti-aircraft and ground targets, it proved to be the finest anti-tank weapon of the campaign in North Africa. General Rommel used these guns to destroy British armor at long range, after using his own armor to draw out the enemy tanks. Behind the Flak 18 is a Krupp Kfz 69 "Protze" light truck. (Bundesarchiv)

The very interesting story begins in Rome. The U.S. Embassy in Rome, while still neutral, had, among its staff, an Italian spy. It was not, it appears, the first time, and eventually the spy succeeded in obtaining the key to the safe where the so-called American "Black Code" was kept for security. The Italians broke into the embassy one night, opened the safe, took photos of the code and replaced it without the Americans being aware of anything amiss. The Italians, being allied with Germany, handed over the code to the Germans who, when they managed to break it, did not return the favor. The opposing generals were aware of each other's plans throughout the North African desert campaign until the Battle of El Alamein. The reason why the British, who deciphered all German and Italian signals, were unable to defeat Rommel quickly is another story. (In the end, he was not defeated on the battlefield but indirectly, by interrupting his supply lines thanks to ULTRA intercepts.) Rommel, in an ongoing clash with Hitler's staff officers, talked about doing something but, actually, in many cases, did something entirely different. While the British could read what his messages said, they were surprised with what he actually did. Wavell knew from Rommel's signal intercepts that the German general would be ready to attack in May 1941, and so reassured his subordinates that their opponent would not be able to attack for a month. However, Rommel launched his attack the next day. That is why, until July 1942, Rommel was better informed. His source, his "reliable source" as he called it, was the American military attaché in Cairo, Colonel Fellers. The colonel had shown a dislike for the British, but they needed the Americans so they

were forced not only to ignore it, but also to give him whatever he asked for so he could send his detailed reports about the British in the Western Desert. Fellers meddled almost everywhere, and then filled in his long reports, accompanied by with mostly pessimistic comments, and sent them to Washington through the Telegraph Company of Egypt. Fellers freely signed his name and sent his reports to just two addresses, as if he wanted to make German interceptions a lot easier. The German signals interception service, E-dienst, had these reports deciphered within a few hours after they had been sent, and Rommel knew each afternoon the British positions of the previous night. Rommel's good fortune was to last until June 1942. The British, meanwhile, suspected that Rommel was in possession of precise information through a leak somewhere in Cairo. They had asked Fellers about the Black Code's safety and security, but he reassured them that everything was totally secure. Suddenly, during a theatrical performance on German radio, its listeners, both German and Allied, were surprised to hear a German actor, playing the part of an... American military attaché in Cairo, saying that he would collect information about the British to send to Washington. ... Thirty-six hours later Rommel had lost his "reliable source!" It is uncertain whether German radio program was the only reason Rommel lost his unintentional informer, but the fact remains that it was a great loss for the German field marshal at the most critical point of operations.

Field Marshal Kesselring's mission in Italy was to assist Rommel in carrying out his mission. Rommel demanded sufficient fuel and ammunition to cover his army's requirements. His requests were intercepted and deciphered by the British, who could not always form a clear picture of his needs, because Rommel always asked for more supplies and materiel than he was liable to get. In consequence, the British overestimated his capabilities while Churchill was always demanding that the British generals attack. Wavell, because he was better informed about the real situation in Rommel's camp, did not comply with Churchill's appeals and was replaced.

Rommel achieved his last amazing victories in 1942 and reached the El Alamein position, albeit exhausted. Churchill sent Field Marshal Alexander against him, while General Montgomery was assigned as the 8th Army's commander. As mentioned earlier, the latter took advantage of ULTRA services, which now had a much more effective staff unlike any time previously.

After his failure to break the British line at Alam Halfa, Hitler recalled Rommel to Germany for health reasons. The British were, through ULTRA, informed of the field marshal's departure on 23 September 1942. On the 24th of the same month, Rommel met Mussolini, who "diagnosed" that his illness was of a psychological nature. The Italian dictator's "diagnosis" was also sent to Hitler and, naturally, to the British. A copy of it was sent to Roosevelt, who commented that Rommel must be in a very awkward position. He further added that Rommel had won all his victories thanks to information intercepted from the British. "Thank God!" he concluded, "this is now over." Apparently, he was referring to Colonel Fellers.

Kesselring, meanwhile, took great care in continuing to send detailed reports for fuel supply shipments to Rommel. In one of his signals, sent a short time before Montgomery launched his great attack at El Alamein, he said: "The tanker 'Proserpina' sails at night on 21 October carrying 2,500 tons of fuel. It will reach Tobruk on the morning of the 26th. Tanker 'Luisiano' ready to sail on the 25th carrying 1,500 tons of fuel. If 'Proserpina' reaches Tobruk, 'Luisiano' will sail with tanker 'Portofino' from Taranto on the night of the 27th, reaching Tobruk around the 31st. 'Portofino' is loaded with 2,200 tons of fuel." The British could not have expected a better description than that!

The British sent reconnaissance aircraft to "locate" the enemy convoy, so as not to reveal their information source. The convoy never reached its destination. Kesselring had suspected something was amiss when the British ships engaged a convoy during a fog-bound day, when air reconnaissance would have been impossible, and asked Abwehr (the German Intelligence Service) to investigate this information leak. The British, after intercepting and deciphering his signal, sent a signal of their own to Naples that could be intercepted by the Germans, congratulating an "agent" of theirs and rewarding him with a bonus. The Germans, assured that their code was secure, assumed that the leak must have originated from an Italian source and accused the Italians of it. Rommel was enjoying time with his family when the British attack was launched and his replacement, General Stumme, disappeared. Within 48 hours after the launch of the attack, Rommel was again in his headquarters. When he realized that the enemy was in control, he decided to withdraw. The British intercepted one of his signals to Hitler,

Rommel retained the initiative in the battles against the British in North Africa until June 1942. Even after June, he managed to exact a heavy price for the victory at El Alamein and then fought a brilliant defensive action in Tunisia. (Bundesarchiv)

describing the reality of the situation and ending: "... in the present situation, the gradual destruction of our army must be considered as inevitable, despite its heroic defense and the troops' high morale." In this signal, he made no mention of his intention to withdraw. By the time Hitler received the signal at his headquarters in East Prussia, the British had already intercepted and deciphered it. Some time later, the head of British intelligence services

passed it to Churchill and to the few officials who had access to intercepted signals. Everyone understood that Rommel was in a very dire situation and was desperately seeking help. This was good news, and Churchill sent it to Eisenhower, who noted it in his diary.

ULTRA staff continued intercepting signals throughout the war, but it took many years for them to be credited with a share of the decisive British victory at El Alamein.

Lesser-known details

Rommel is shown here in discussions with an Italian commander. In North Africa, Rommel was in the difficult position of being subordinate to both his own high command as well as to the Italians who supplied the majority of the Axis force, but whom he held in no great esteem.

Lesser-known aspects of the Battle of El Alamein

- Rommel's reputation, due to his outstanding victories, was so great among friend and foe alike that General Auchinleck was forced to order the 8th Army officers to use words like "the enemy" or "the opponent" when referring to the Germans. Otherwise, he felt Rommel would receive indirect credit that, ultimately, would be bad for the Allied morale. Auchinleck ended this order with a characteristic postscript: "I do not envy Rommel."
- Saving Egypt, and the turning point of the war in the desert, was judged by many to be due to Auchinleck's victory at the First Battle of El Alamein in July 1942 rather than by Montgomery's much-trumpeted methodical battle.
- On the wall of his command vehicle, Montgomery had two pictures of Rommel to constantly remind him of the capable enemy he was facing. As far as is known, the "Desert Fox" did not return this compliment!
- General Georg Stumme had been Commanding Officer 40th Panzer Corps in 1941, during von List's 12th Army invasion of Greece and Yugoslavia. This formation outflanked the "Metaxas Line," captured Thessaloniki, and cut off the Greek army on the Albanian Front. However, Stumme fell from grace in 1942 when one of his ADCs was captured by the Soviets with all the corps' operational plans on him.
- General Ritter von Thoma was a Wehrmacht observer during the Spanish Civil War. He was an ardent student of armored force operations. At El Alamein he was unfortunate enough to be captured by the British.
- In his heart, Rommel never believed that the Axis could ever win in Africa after the United States entered the war. "If the Americans manage to land somewhere on the African continent, it will be just a matter of time before we are sent back to Europe," he said.
- Just a little under three weeks prior to the Battle of El Alamein, the Luftwaffe lost, through a tragic flying accident, the only man whose reputation and medals were comparable to Rommel's in Africa. He was the 23-year-old fighter pilot Hans-Joachim Marseille, the only pilot in history credited with 158 RAF aircraft.
- British SAS troops used, at least once, the Qatarra Depression to infiltrate the Axis rear unobserved on a sabotage mission.
- To boost his troops' morale, Stumme held many odd events before the Battle of El Alamein. For example, a party was held to commemorate the 4 millionth loaf of bread made by the 15th Panzer Division bakers!
- When Goering was

Lesser-known details

informed that the new American anti-tank easily penetrated the panzers' armor, he exclaimed: "Impossible! The Americans only know to make razor blades!"

● When he learned of his promotion to field marshal by Hitler, Rommel's comment was, "I would prefer to have been given another panzer division instead of the field marshal's baton."

● In spite of the threat hanging over Cairo, the city's stock exchange continued working as usual. Indeed, one could follow the course of the battle by simply watching the stock price indicator.

● Canned food used by the Afrika Korps was Italian with the letters "AM" (Amministrazione Militare) stamped on the containers. The German troops derisively translated it as "Alter Mann," the ancient man.

● The heaviest tank that fought at El Alamein was the British Churchill at 39 tons, which made its rather problematic debut. In contrast, the lightest one was the German PzKpfw II at 9.5 tons, which had been in service with the Wehrmacht since 1936!

● With his wife dead, Montgomery's last concern before leaving for Egypt was to ask the school director where his son studied to take care of the boy within his own family until he returned.

● Temperatures in the desert could vary by 60 degrees Centigrade in 24 hours, and the "khamsin" wind that blew at speeds reaching 150 kph created such an electromagnetic disturbance that compasses "went crazy." These strange atmospheric conditions were held responsible for an ammunition depot exploding.

● Lack of water caused the troops to clean their clothes by rubbing them with sand or petrol. If sweat remained on the clothes for too long, the uniforms became so stiff that movement was seriously inhibited.

● The major German invention in the desert war was the 4.5-gallon container for carrying water or fuel. The British enthusiastically adopted them, giving them the soubriquet "jerry can." ("Jerry" was a slang-term for German troops during World War II.)

● In October 1942, 40 percent of all Axis shipping was sunk or seriously damaged by air and naval forces based on Malta while en route to Libya.

● Mussolini never had the opportunity to enter Cairo in triumph as a victor like he had planned. The spirited white horse waiting for him in Africa for that very moment was "captured" by the British, among the other spoils of war after El Alamein.

One of the most notable German air aces of the North African campaign and, indeed, of the war, was Joachim Marseille, seen here as a lieutenant with 3/JG 27 in March 1942. His aircraft was a Bf 109F-4 Trop.

The rival commanders

A weary-looking Rommel gives instructions to one of his officers. By the late summer of 1942, Rommel was clearly exhausted and ill. In fact, when the Allies launched their attack at El Alamein, he had returned to Germany for medical treatment, an example of how well the Allies had concealed their plans.

Field Marshal Erwin Rommel, "The Desert Fox" (1891-1944)

Erwin Johannes Eugen Rommel was born on 15 November 1891 at Heidenheim, close to the town of Ulm. He was one of four children, three boys and a girl, of Erwin and Helene Rommel. His father was head of a junior high school, and he taught Rommel his first letters. When Rommel was young he displayed a technical aptitude, but his father urged him to take up a military profession.

More then 60 years after his death, field marshal Erwin Rommel retains the glamour of one of the greatest battle leaders, as he was daring, aggressive, and fully knowledgeable of the techniques of modern war.

Rommel distinguished himself during World War I. He was awarded the Iron Cross, First and Second Class, on the Western Front and the highest military medal, Pour le Mérite, on the Italian Front. By the time the war ended, he was a captain. He married in 1916 after falling in love with Lucie, who bore him a son, Manfred. They lived happily for many years. In 1935, he became an instructor at the Potsdam War Academy. It was there that he wrote his first and only book, Infantry Attacks (Infanterie greift an), an excellent infantry tactics manual based on his World War I experiences. In fact, Hitler, after reading the book, expressed some highly complimentary comments about its author.

On 10th May 1940, Rommel led the 7th Panzer Division, known as the "Ghost Division," during the invasion of France, where he particularly distinguished himself. By the end of the campaign Rommel had become a hero in Germany. Hitler awarded him the Iron Cross, and Nazi propaganda portrayed him as a typical

"product" of the Third Reich. The following year, following the crushing defeat of the Italians in Cyrenaica, Hitler gave Rommel command of a small force, the Deutsches Afrika Korps, in Libya. Over the next 18 months, his reputation as the world's foremost armored force commander swept around the globe. Rommel reached the peak of his career in the summer of 1942, when he defeated the 8th Army between Gazala and Tobruk and pursued its remnants to the Nile Delta. Churchill himself acknowledged his merit in the House of Commons. For his success, Hitler promoted him to field marshal. However, by this time, the Fuhrer had turned all his attention to the campaign in Russia, directing all his forces and efforts there. Rommel, therefore, found himself in a game that was lost before it had hardly begun. His health suffered, he lacked the vital supplies for the North African front, and Allied air superiority was crushing. So, when the new British leadership of Alexander and Montgomery launched its

The rival commanders

attack at El Alamein, the line that Rommel had tried in vain to break through during his last attack, there was nothing for him to do but to withdraw, and this retreat was very long ... 2,400 kilometers long. While this was taking place, the Axis forces found themselves fighting on two fronts following the American landings in Algeria. Holding the Mersa Brega line "at all costs" was impossible, despite Hitler's demands. Rommel paid Hitler a visit and suggested the evacuation of North Africa. This suggestion, however, sent the Fuhrer into a towering rage and his intractable stance shook Rommel's faith in him, a faith that was unquestioned until then. He returned to Africa to discover that the British and Americans were preparing a joint two-pronged attack. He succeeded in withdrawing, without being discovered, to man positions 400 kilometers to the west. He scored his last victory against the Americans at the Battle of Kasserine Pass. This victory considerably delayed the overall Allied victory in North Africa. However, by this time, North Africa was of no consequence for Hitler, who recalled Rommel from the North African front in order to save his prestige and have him in reserve, ready for another command.

Rommel won victories with fewer forces and without air superiority, a feat that no other general, Allied or Axis, managed. Of course, he made mistakes, but this was unavoidable when fighting against superior odds. He was always in the vanguard, but gave many younger officers the chance to distinguish their selves and they idolized him for it. His behavior towards prisoners of war was impeccable, and his departure from North Africa made his opponents feel sorry as he was held in high esteem as a worthy adversary. Rommel remained out of action for some considerable time, during which he managed to take an extended leave with his family. Finally, he was given command of an army group in northern Italy, where an Allied landing was expected. When that threat was proven to be unfounded, he was entrusted with the command of the Atlantic Wall, to drive back the expected Allied landing sometime in the future. The plan Rommel proposed for the defense of north-west Europe was hailed as an "extremely well-thought-out strategy but unappreciated neither by the Wehrmacht High Command, nor by von Rundstedt himself." Rommel, correctly, emphasized that the only hope for the Germans would be to halt the invaders

on the beaches and for the landing to fail. Rommel realized that the game was up a few days after the landings when the Allies had secured a beachhead. Soon after, while being driven to his headquarters his car was strafed by an Allied fighter, and he was slightly injured. He survived his wounds but, while at home recuperating, was visited by two generals from Berlin. Rommel had become one of the targets of Hitler's revenge for the 20 July 1944 attempt on his life. It seems that during an interrogation someone broke and mentioned the field marshal's name. Rommel was popular and a trial in the Peoples' Court, the fate of all other plotters, would have been embarrassing to the regime. So a compromise was found and the two visitors presented Rommel with the dilemma "trial or suicide," adding that, if he chose the latter, his family would be fully cared for. Rommel opted for suicide by poison and died with his legend still intact.

Rommel was a simple, talented, and patriotic German officer, a charismatic leader, a master of tactics and maneuver, a frontline officer who commanded by example, but he, like many others, became involved in the chaos of the Third Reich.

The rival commanders

Lieutenant General Montgomery during the Battle of El Alamein. He wears an Australian fur felt slouch hat with the badges of all the units under his command.

Many historians, undoubtedly, consider Montgomery, or Monty as he became known, to be the greatest British general after Wellington. This was due to his high level of professionalism and sense of equilibrium rather than for the fact that he was disdainful and arrogant in his relationship with his contemporary generals, especially the Americans!

Field Marshal Bernard Law Montgomery (1887-1976)

Monty came from an Irish family and was the fourth of nine children born to his despotic mother. He followed the military profession (he graduated 36th out of a total of 170 students from the Royal Military Academy, Sandhurst, in 1908) and his baptism by fire, almost fatal, was during the First Battle of Ypres in October 1914. He was so badly wounded that his name was even placed on the register of killed troops and officers! Montgomery was awarded an unusually high medal for his rank, the DSO, for participating in this battle. His wound in the lung caused him to develop a deep aversion to smoking, while the horrendous casualties the British sustained during World War I made him very cautious, perhaps overly so, as a commander during World War II. For the first reason, he came into conflict with Eisenhower who was a chain-smoker, while Patton mocked him for the second reason and also despised him.

The rival commanders

His incompatibility with the professional standards in the British Army during the interwar years cost him further promotion. In 1927, at the age of 39, he married a war widow, but she tragically died in 1938 from a rare blood infection. Monty never overcame this loss, and devoted himself instead to preparing the British Army for the approaching conflict.

Monty was commanding officer of a select British division, the 3rd, and he led it intact to England following the Dunkirk evacuation. He remained in Britain for two more years, where he used his prodigious energy to train British troops in new tactics. After Rommel defeated the 8th Army in North Africa, Montgomery was put forward as its replacement commander, but Churchill chose General Gott instead. Gott unfortunately was killed on his way to take over his new command, so Monty took command of the 8th Army. On presenting himself to Field Marshal Alexander on his way to his new position, "Alex" gave him a simple order: "Go into the desert and defeat Rommel!" Monty took over the 8th Army determined to do just that.

Montgomery's victory at the Battle of El Alamein was the first great Allied victory against Hitler's Reich, and it caused a storm of elation.

Monty became popular in both Britain and America. It appears, naturally enough, that his popularity went to his head making him somewhat arrogant to his superiors and contemporaries. However, one of his great attributes was that he also took advantage of this popularity to instill an esprit de corps in his troops and to raise their morale like no other World War II commander.

After the final defeat of the Axis forces in North Africa, Monty with his 8th Army landed in Sicily and then went on into mainland Italy. During this time, his relationship with the American generals, especially Patton and Bradley, deteriorated. He then devoted himself to preparing for the Normandy invasion.

Montgomery's contribution to the Normandy landings was that he insisted on eight of eight divisions taking part, three of them being airborne, and on him being given made ground forces commander under Eisenhower, who was supreme allied commander. It took very little time for friction to develop between him and the American generals, although his basic strategy of continuously wearing down the enemy on the front's left flank and then to break out on the right was what ultimately won the Normandy battle. Additionally, his relations with Eisenhower, ideal until

September 1944, were overshadowed when Eisenhower assumed overall command. Montgomery's only defeat, in the Arnhem airborne landings, gave his American detractors the chance to make malicious and disparaging comments. Monty returned the compliment just as caustically after the American mishap in the Ardennes in December 1944, when he was almost relieved of his duties after stating that he had helped the Americans survive the disaster that they had initiated by not following his strategy! It appears that Churchill was totally accurate in characterizing Monty as "fearless during retreat, invincible during the advance, unbearable during victory!"

Monty became chief of the Imperial General Staff after 1945. In January 1946 he was created 1st Viscount Montgomery of Alamein and, in December of the same year, raised to Knight of the Garter. For a time he was deputy supreme allied commander Europe, Eisenhower's second-in-command in NATO, but the rift between them was unbridgeable as they were poles apart. And, indeed, it widened following the publication of their memoirs.

First Viscount Montgomery of Alamein died, aged 89, in 1976, still believing in the personal myth about his name.

Bibliography

1. *Afrika Korps*, Time-Life Books, 1991.
2. C. Barnett, *Hitler's Generals*, Grove Weidenfeld, 1989.
3. C. Barnett, *The Desert Generals*, 1999.
4. D. Boyle, *World War II: A Photographic History*, Barnes & Noble, 1998.
5. R. Cartier, I Istoria toy Defterou Pagosmiou Polemou, Papyros (La Seconde Guerre Mondiale), 1964 (In the Greek language).
6. M. Croll, *The History of Landmines*, Leo Cooper, 1998.
7. T. Donnelly & S. Naylor, *Clash of Chariots*, Berkely, 1996.
8. H.G. von Esebeck, *Rommel*, Damianos, 1960 (In the Greek language).
9. F. Kurowski, *Knight's Cross Holders of the Afrika Korps*, Schiffer Publishing, 1996.
10. K. Macksey, *Rommel: His Battles and Campaigns*, Da Capo Press, 1997.
11. D. McGuirk, *Rommel's Army in Africa*, Airlife Publishing, 1987.
12. A. Moorehead, *African Trilogy*, Casell, 1998.
13. S. Rothwell, "The evolution of British armor doctrine," *Command* magazine Issue 52.
14. H. Scheibert, *Kampf und Undergang der Deutschen Panzertruppe*, 1939-1945, Podzun Pallas, 1992.
15. *The War in Desert*, Time-Life Books, 1999.
16. Karl Hecks, *Bombing 1939-45: The Air Offensive against Land targets in World War II*, Robert Hale Ltd., 1990.
17. Phillips C. E. Lucas, *Alamein*, William Heineman Ltd., 1962.
18. Francis K. Mason, "Air War Over the Desert", *Wings of Fame*, Vol. 10, 1999.
19. Giovanni and Giorgio Apostolo Massimello, *Italian Aces of World War 2*, Osprey Publishing Ltd., 2000.
20. Hans Werner Neulen, *In the Skies of Europe – Air Forces Allied to the Luftwaffe 1939-1945*, The Crowood Press, 1998.
21. Alexander and Ferdinando D'Amico Pramstrahle, ALI ITALIANE (ITALIAN WINGS), August 2000 (Internet).
22. Jerry Scutts, *Bf 109 Aces of North Africa and the Mediterranean*, Osprey Publishing Ltd., 1994.
23. Mike Spick, *Allied Fighter Aces of World War II*, Greenhill Books, 1997.
24. Hans-Gunther Stark, DAS DEUTSCHE AFRIKA-KORPS (Internet).
25. University of North Carolina, AIRCRAFT DATA (Internet).
26. John Weal, *Messerschmitt Bf 110 Zerstörer Aces of World War 2*, Osprey Publishing Ltd, 1998.
27. *Afrika Korps*, Histoire & Collections, 1994.
28. Christopher Ailsby, *World War 2 German Medals*, Ian Allan Publishing, 1994.
29. *Allied Soldiers of World War II*, Histoire & Collections, 1994.
30. Andrew Cormack, *The Royal Air Force 1939-45*, Osprey Books, 1990.
31. *German Soldiers of World War II*, Histoire & Collections, 1994.
32. Jorg Hormann, *German Uniforms of the 20th Century I & II*, Schiffer Publishing, 1989.
33. Andrew Mollo, *The Armed Forces of WW II*, Orbis Publishing, 1981.
34. John Laffin, *The Australian Army at War*, Osprey Books, 1982.
35. *Polemikes Epihireisis ke Antifasistikos Agonas stin Mesi Anatoli (Military Operations and Anti-fascist Struggle in the Middle East,)* PSAMA, 1986 (In the Greek language).
36. Guido Rosignoli, Army Badges & Insignia of World War 2, Blandford Press, 1972.
37. Guido Rosignoli, *Army Uniforms of World War 2*, Blandford Press, 1973.
38. Kevin Conley Ruffner, *Luftwaffe Field Divisions 1941-45*, Osprey Books, 1990.
39. Jan Sumner, *The French Army 1939-45 (2)*, Osprey Books, 1998.
40. Rex Tyre, *Mussolini's Soldiers*, Airlife Publishing, 1995.
41. Nigel Thomas, *Foreign Volunteers of the Allied Forces*, Osprey Books, 1991.
42. Nigel Thomas, *The German Army 1939-45 (2)*, Osprey Books, 1998.
43. Gordon Williamson, *Afrikacorps 1941-43*, Osprey Books, 1991.
44. Mick J. Prodger, *Luftwaffe vs. RAF*, Atglen, Schiffer, 1997.
45. Christopher Chant, *The Tank*, London, Patrick Stephens, 1994.
46. Christopher F. Foss, *Tanks & Fighting Vehicles*, London, Salamander, 1997.
47. Peter Gudgin, *Armoured Firepower*, London, Sutton Publishing, 1977.

48. Ian V. Hogg, *Allied Armour of World War II,* London, Crowood Press, 2000.

49. Volkmar Kuehn, *Rommel in the Desert*, West Chester, Schiffer, 1991.

50. Thomas Lentz, *Tank Combat in North Africa*, West Chester, Schiffer, 1998.

51. James Lucas, *War in the Desert*, New York, Beaufort Books, 1982.

52. John Mac Donald, *Great Battles of World War II*, London, Marshall Editions, 1986.

53. Kenneth Macksey, *Tank Versus Tank*, London, Magna Books, 1991.

54. Bryan Perret, *British Tanks in North Africa*, London, Osprey, 1981.

55. Bryan Perret, *Tank Warfare*, London, Patrick Stephens, 1988.

56. Various monographs: Osprey New Vanguard, Squadron/Signal In Action.

57. R.J. Bender and R.D. Law, *Afrika Korps*, London Press.

58. *After the Battle*, After the Battle prints, 1976.

59. P. Karykas, S. Kaparis, I. Hondromatidis, *Rommel, O Thrylos tis Erimou (Rommel, the Desert Legend)*, Athens, Periskopio, 1999 (In the Greek language).

60. J. Piekalkiewicz, *The Air War 1939-1945*, Poole, Blandord Press.

61. R. Cartier, *I Istoria tou Defterou Pagosmiou Polemou Volume B' (La Seconde Guerre Mondiale)*, 1995 (In the Greek language).

62. M. Carver, *El Alamein*, London, 1962.

63. DIS/GES Publications, *O Ellinikos Stratos sti Mesi Anatoli 1941-1945 (The Greek Army in the Middle East 1941-1945)*, 1995 (In the Greek language).

64. Pafsania Katsota, *I Dekaetia 1940-1950 (The decade 1940-1950)*, 1981 (In the Greek language).

65. Ger. Lamarc, *Ellinikon Aima is Afrikin – Italian – Aigeon (Greek Blood in Africa – Italy – The Aegean)*, 1978 (In the Greek language).

66. Basil Liddell Hart, *Istoria tou Defetrou Pagosmiou Polemou Volume 2 (History of the Second World War)*, 1977 (In the Greek language).

67. I. Manetas, *Mahomeni Ellas 1942-1945 Volume A' (Greece Fighting 1942-1945)*, 1979 (In the Greek language).

68. *Ta Apomnimonevmata tou Stratarhou Montgomery (Field Marshal Montgomery's Memoirs)*, Atlas 1960 (In the Greek language).

69. Sof. Tzanetis, *Taxiarhia El-Alamein (El-Alamein Brigade)*, 1977 (In the Greek language).

70. D. Young, *Rommel*, GES Editions, 1982 (In the Greek language).

71. David Irving, *The Trail of the Fox*, New York, Avon Books, 1978.

72. *The Secret War*, Alexandria, Time-Life, 1981.

73. John Toland, *Hitler*, New York, Ballantine Books, 1976.

74. G. L. Weinberg, *A World at Arms*, Cambridge, University of Cambridge, 1994.